GRAPHIS STUDENT DESIGN 96

Treasures

Sometimes, judging

from the outside, you

would never guess how

mysteriously beautiful

the inside can be.

GRAPHIS STUDENT DESIGN 96

THE INTERNATIONAL ANNUAL OF DESIGN AND COMMUNICATION BY STUDENTS

DAS INTERNATIONALE JAHRBUCH ÜBER KOMMUNIKATIONSDESIGN VON STUDENTEN

UN RÉPERTOIRE INTERNATIONAL DE PROJETS D'EXPRESSION VISUELLE D'ÉTUDIANTS

EDITED BY · HERAUSGEGEBEN VON · EDITÉ PAR:

B. MARTIN PEDERSEN

PUBLISHER AND CREATIVE DIRECTOR: B. MARTIN PEDERSEN

EDITORS: HEINKE JENSSEN, ANNETTE CRANDALL

ASSISTANT EDITOR: JÖRG REIMANN

ART DIRECTORS: B. MARTIN PEDERSEN, JENNIFER THORPE

GRAPHIS U.S., INC., NEW YORK AND

GRAPHIS PRESS CORP. ZÜRICH (SWITZERLAND)

CONTENTS · INHALT · SOMMAIRE

REMARKS

WE EXTEND OUR HEARTFELT THANKS TO CONTRIBUTORS THROUGHOUT THE WORLD WHO HAVE MADE IT POSSIBLE TO PUBLISH A WIDE AND INTERNATIONAL SPECTRUM OF THE BEST WORK IN THIS FIELD.

ENTRY INSTRUCTIONS FOR NEXT YEAR'S ANNUAL MAY BE REQUESTED AT:
GRAPHIS PRESS
141 LEXINGTON AVENUE
NEW YORK, NY 10016-8193

ANMERKUNGEN

UNSER DANK GILT DEN EINSENDERN AUS ALLER WELT, DIE ES UNS DURCH IHRE BEITRÄGE ERMÖGLICHT HABEN, EIN BREITES, INTERNATIONALES SPEKTRUM DER BESTEN ARBEITEN ZU VERÖFFENTLICHEN.

TEILNAHMEBEDINGUNGEN FÜR DAS NÄCHSTE JAHRBUCH SIND ERHÄLTLICH BEIM:
GRAPHIS VERLAG AG
DUFOURSTRASSE 107
8008 ZÜRICH, SCHWEIZ

REMERCIEMENTS

NOUS REMERCIONS LES PARTICIPANTS DU MONDE ENTIER QUI ONT RENDU POSSIBLE LA PUBLICATION DE CET OUVRAGE OFFRANT UN PANORAMA COMPLET DES MEILLEURS TRAVAUX RÉALISÉS DANS CE DOMAINE.

LES MODALITÉS D'INSCRIPTION PEUVENT ÊTRE OBTENUES AUPRÈS DE:
EDITIONS GRAPHIS
DUFOURSTRASSE 107
8008 ZÜRICH, SUISSE

(PHOTO PRECEDING SPREAD) STUDENT: JOAN FOLKMAN COLLEGE: CALIFORNIA COLLEGE OF ARTS AND CRAFTS DEGREE: BFA IN GRAPHIC DESIGN PROFESSOR: MICHAEL VANDERBYL COUNTRY: USA ■ (THIS SPREAD) STUDENT: YESMIN CHAN COLLEGE: UNIVERSITY OF NORTHUMBRIA DEGREE: MA IN DESIGN COUNTRY: GREAT BRITAIN

GRAPHIS PUBLICATIONS

GRAPHIS, THE INTERNATIONAL BI-MONTHLY JOURNAL OF VISUAL COMMUNICATION
GRAPHIS SHOPPING BAG, AN INTERNATIONAL COLLECTION OF SHOPPING BAG DESIGN
GRAPHIS MUSIC CD, AN INTERNATIONAL COLLECTION OF CD DESIGN
GRAPHIS BOOK DESIGN, AN INTERNATIONAL COLLECTION OF BOOK DESIGN
GRAPHIS DESIGN, THE INTERNATIONAL ANNUAL OF DESIGN AND ILLUSTRATION
GRAPHIS ADVERTISING, THE INTERNATIONAL ANNUAL OF ADVERTISING
GRAPHIS BROCHURES, A COMPILATION OF BROCHURE DESIGN
GRAPHIS PHOTO, THE INTERNATIONAL ANNUAL OF PHOTOGRAPHY
GRAPHIS ALTERNATIVE PHOTOGRAPHY, THE INTERNATIONAL ANNUAL OF ALTERNATIVE PHOTOGRAPHY
GRAPHIS NUDES, A COLLECTION OF CAREFULLY SELECTED SOPHISTICATED IMAGES
GRAPHIS POSTER, THE INTERNATIONAL ANNUAL OF POSTER ART
GRAPHIS PACKAGING, AN INTERNATIONAL COMPILATION OF PACKAGING DESIGN
GRAPHIS LETTERHEAD, AN INTERNATIONAL COMPILATION OF LETTERHEAD DESIGN
GRAPHIS DIAGRAM, THE GRAPHIC VISUALIZATION OF ABSTRACT, TECHNICAL AND STATISTICAL FACTS AND FUNCTIONS
GRAPHIS LOGO, AN INTERNATIONAL COMPILATION OF LOGOS
GRAPHIS EPHEMERA, AN INTERNATIONAL COLLECTION OF PROMOTIONAL ART
GRAPHIS PUBLICATION, AN INTERNATIONAL SURVEY OF THE BEST IN MAGAZINE DESIGN
GRAPHIS ANNUAL REPORTS, AN INTERNATIONAL COMPILATION OF THE BEST DESIGNED ANNUAL REPORTS
GRAPHIS CORPORATE IDENTITY, AN INTERNATIONAL COMPILATION OF THE BEST IN CORPORATE IDENTITY DESIGN
GRAPHIS TYPOGRAPHY, AN INTERNATIONAL COMPILATION OF THE BEST IN TYPOGRAPHIC DESIGN

GRAPHIS PUBLIKATIONEN

GRAPHIS, DIE INTERNATIONALE ZWEIMONATSZEITSCHRIFT DER VISUELLEN KOMMUNIKATION
GRAPHIS SHOPPING BAG, TRAGTASCHEN-DESIGN IM INTERNATIONALEN ÜBERBLICK
GRAPHIS MUSIC CD, CD-DESIGN IM INTERNATIONALEN ÜBERBLICK
GRAPHIS BOOKS, BUCHGESTALTUNG IM INTERNATIONALEN ÜBERBLICK
GRAPHIS DESIGN, DAS INTERNATIONALE JAHRBUCH ÜBER DESIGN UND ILLUSTRATION
GRAPHIS ADVERTISING, DAS INTERNATIONALE JAHRBUCH DER WERBUNG
GRAPHIS BROCHURES, BROSCHÜRENDESIGN IM INTERNATIONAL ÜBERBLICK
GRAPHIS PHOTO, DAS INTERNATIONALE JAHRBUCH DER PHOTOGRAPHIE
GRAPHIS ALTERNATIVE PHOTOGRAPHY, DAS INTERNATIONALE JAHRBUCH ÜBER ALTERNATIVE PHOTOGRAPHIE
GRAPHIS NUDES, EINE SAMMLUNG SORGFÄLTIG AUSGEWÄHLTER AKTPHOTOGRAPHIE
GRAPHIS POSTER, DAS INTERNATIONALE JAHRBUCH DER PLAKATKUNST
GRAPHIS PACKAGING, EIN INTERNATIONALER ÜBERBLICK ÜBER DIE PACKUNGSGESTALTUNG
GRAPHIS LETTERHEAD, EIN INTERNATIONALER ÜBERBLICK ÜBER BRIEFPAPIERGESTALTUNG
GRAPHIS DIAGRAM, DIE GRAPHISCHE DARSTELLUNG ABSTRAKTER TECHNISCHER UND STATISTISCHER DATEN UND FAKTEN
GRAPHIS LOGO, EINE INTERNATIONALE AUSWAHL VON FIRMEN-LOGOS
GRAPHIS EPHEMERA, EINE INTERNATIONALE SAMMLUNG GRAPHISCHER DOKUMENTE DES TÄGLICHEN LEBENS
GRAPHIS MAGAZINDESIGN, EINE INTERNATIONALE ZUSAMMENSTELLUNG DES BESTEN ZEITSCHRIFTEN-DESIGNS
GRAPHIS ANNUAL REPORTS, EIN INTERNATIONALER ÜBERBLICK ÜBER DIE GESTALTUNG VON JAHRESBERICHTEN
GRAPHIS CORPORATE IDENTITY, EINE INTERNATIONALE AUSWAHL DES BESTEN CORPORATE IDENTITY DESIGNS
GRAPHIS TYPOGRAPHY, EINE INTERNATIONALE ZUSAMMENSTELLUNG DES BESTEN TYPOGRAPHIE DESIGN

PUBLICATIONS GRAPHIS

GRAPHIS, LA REVUE BIMESTRIELLE INTERNATIONALE DE LA COMMUNICATION VISUELLE
GRAPHIS SHOPPING BAG, UNE COMPILATION INTERNATIONALE SUR LE DESIGN DES SACS À COMMISSIONS
GRAPHIS MUSIC CD, UNE COMPILATION INTERNATIONALE SUR LE DESIGN DES CD
GRAPHIS BOOKS, UNE COMPILATION INTERNATIONALE SUR LE DESIGN DES LIVRES
GRAPHIS DESIGN, LE RÉPERTOIRE INTERNATIONAL DE LA COMMUNICATION VISUELLE
GRAPHIS ADVERTISING, LE RÉPERTOIRE INTERNATIONAL DE LA PUBLICITÉ
GRAPHIS BROCHURES, UNE COMPILATION INTERNATIONALE SUR LE DESIGN DES BROCHURES
GRAPHIS PHOTO, LE RÉPERTOIRE INTERNATIONAL DE LA PHOTOGRAPHIE
GRAPHIS ALTERNATIVE PHOTOGRAPHY, LE RÉPERTOIRE INTERNATIONAL DE LA PHOTOGRAPHIE ALTERNATIVE
GRAPHIS NUDES, UN FLORILÈGE DE LA PHOTOGRAPHIE DE NUS
GRAPHIS POSTER, LE RÉPERTOIRE INTERNATIONAL DE L'AFFICHE
GRAPHIS PACKAGING, LE RÉPERTOIRE INTERNATIONAL DE LA CRÉATION D'EMBALLAGES
GRAPHIS LETTERHEAD, LE RÉPERTOIRE INTERNATIONAL DU DESIGN DE PAPIER À LETTRES
GRAPHIS DIAGRAM, LE RÉPERTOIRE GRAPHIQUE DE FAITS ET DONNÉES ABSTRAITS, TECHNIQUES ET STATISTIQUES
GRAPHIS LOGO, LE RÉPERTOIRE INTERNATIONAL DU LOGO
GRAPHIS EPHEMERA, LE GRAPHISME – UN ÉTAT D'ESPRIT AU QUOTIDIEN
GRAPHIS PUBLICATION, LE RÉPERTOIRE INTERNATIONAL DU DESIGN DE PÉRIODIQUES
GRAPHIS ANNUAL REPORTS, PANORAMA INTERNATIONAL DU MEILLEUR DESIGN DE RAPPORTS ANNUELS D'ENTREPRISES
GRAPHIS CORPORATE IDENTITY, PANORAMA INTERNATIONAL DU MEILLEUR DESIGN D'IDENTITÉ CORPORATE
GRAPHIS TYPOGRAPHY, LE RÉPERTOIRE INTERNATIONAL DU MEILLEUR DESIGN DE TYPOGRAPHIE

PUBLICATION NO. 261 (ISBN 1-888001-01-1)
© COPYRIGHT UNDER UNIVERSAL COPYRIGHT CONVENTION
COPYRIGHT © 1996 BY GRAPHIS U.S., NEW YORK, GRAPHIS PRESS CORP., ZURICH, SWITZERLAND
JACKET AND BOOK DESIGN COPYRIGHT © 1996 BY PEDERSEN DESIGN
141 LEXINGTON AVENUE, NEW YORK, N.Y. 10016 USA

PRINTED IN HONG KONG BY PARAMOUNT PRINTING COMPANY LIMITED

COMMENTARY BY B. MARTIN PEDERSEN

This annual is dedicated to the education community and especially to those gifted teachers who have the ability to somehow touch a student's inspirational chords. I would like to express my gratitude to Chris Hill from The Hill Group in Texas, who inspired this long overdue book, along with Steven Holt of frogdesign in California. Additonal thanks go to Ken Cato from Cato Design, Australia, Professor Uwe Loesch from the Bergischen Universität Wuppertal, Germany, Rebeca Méndez from the Art Center College of Design in Pasadena, California, Michael Vanderbyl, Dean of the California College of Arts & Crafts in San Francisco, California, and my AGI colleagues for their dedication to education. Also my thanks to Professor Olaf Leu from the Fachhochschule Rheinland-Pfalz, Mainz, Germany, for his endless enthusiasm and support to both the education community and to me over the years.

Dieses Buch ist den Lehrinstituten und ganz besonders jenen Pädagogen gewidmet, die die Fähigkeit haben, ihre Schüler zu inspirieren. Mein besonderer Dank geht an Chris Hill von The Hill Group, Texas, der die Anregung zu diesem längst überfälligen Buch gab, und an Steven Holt von frogdesign in Kalifornien. Mein Dank gilt ausserdem Ken Cato von Cato Design, Australien, Professor Uwe Loesch von der Bergischen Universität Wuppertal, Rebeca Méndez vom Art Center College of Design in Pasadena, Kalifornien, und Michael Vanderbyl, Dekan des California College of Arts & Crafts in San Francisco, Kalifornien, sowie meinen AGI-Kollegen für ihr Engagement im Lehrbereich. Professor Olaf Leu von der Fachhochschule Rheinland-Pfalz, Mainz, danke ich für seinen unermüdlichen Enthusiasmus und seine jahrelange Unterstützung und seinen Einsatz für die Ausbildung des Nachwuchses.

Ce livre annuel s'adresse à la communauté des enseignants et tout spécialement à ceux de ses membres qui ont le don de faire vibrer chez l'étudiant la corde de la créativité. Je tiens à exprimer toute ma gratitude à Chris Hill de The Hill Group, Texas, qui est l'inspirateur de ce livre tant attendu, ainsi qu'à Steven Holt, de frogdesign, en Californie. Mes remerciements vont également à Ken Cato, de Cato Design, Australie, au professeur Uwe Loesch, de la Bergischen Universität Wuppertal, Allemagne, à Rebeca Mendez du Art Center College of Design à Pasadena, Californie, et à Michael Vanderbyl, doyen du California College of Arts & Crafts de San Francisco, Californie, ainsi quà mes collègues de l'AGI pour leur dévouement à la cause de l'enseignement. Je remercie enfin le Professeur Olaf Leu de la Fachhochschule Rheinland-Pfalz, Mainz, pour l'enthousiasme et le soutien dont il m'entoure depuis tant années.

Building the Confidence to Explore BY KEN CATO

Starting a course in design is the first step in a never-ending journey. It is a learning experience that brings great joy, pleasure, and value, as well as some frustration to the lives of those who embark upon it. Hopefully the results also bring joy to those who encounter them. Of course there have been many gifted and intuitive people who have made their way without formal training to the top of our profession, but for most of us our formal education began at a university or design school. □ The traditions of the design education system are still relevant, but new technology and new media are affecting the way we work and presenting new opportunities. The "computer factor" has required many established design companies to rethink the way they are structured and the way they work. The business community, and its relationship to design, have also changed. Business leaders are beginning to acknowledge the strategic and communicative values of design which can dramatically affect company performance. □ With these two emerging phenomena in mind, what kind of designers do universities and design colleges need to develop? The ideal design student is one who is curious to explore lateral thinking, who has sensitivity, style, and aesthetic intuition, plus the ability to communicate and convince clients that good design equals good communication. □ We have all heard the maxim "rubbish in, rubbish out." This is what we must remember when we consider who we wish to attract into design courses. Students are often steered into them because they are not suited to science, medicine, or finance, but they can draw. But talent alone is never enough—very often people with limited abilities simply work harder. Attracting the right person, however, is still the starting point. □ I have always believed that a broad range of subjects and design skills, taught in the early stages of the course, produces a designer with the confidence to explore broad-based solutions and to take on new challenges. Of course, one must take the student's personality into account. Design is not about doing things one way. A number of approaches may be relevant, but what distinguishes a project is the individual vision and approach of the designer. □ Our profession has come a long way in assisting today's young professionals. We must continue to encourage universities and design schools to provide substantial student contact with practicing designers. I believe the broader the range of professionals with whom students interact, the more open young minds will be. There are now several annual conferences such as the Icograda Conference in London and the IDEAS Student Design Conference in Melbourne which provide students with the opportunity to experience the different styles of practicing designers. □ In general, students spend little time with international designers—but maintaining fresh input is critical. Shorter course hours and the pressure to learn a broader range of skills in a reduced period of time have led to some very unpalatable choices. While I recognize the significance of technological development and the opportunities that it brings, the basics must still be taught. Our future designers must learn to work as not just part of the design team, but as part of a broader network of clients and other design practitioners including architects, interior designers, fashion designers, etc. □ I believe we must cultivate those who are not necessarily designers, but who still appreciate design. One sure way of having better design work in our community is by educating those who will purchase the work. The need for design managers within the business community is obvious—we all want our clients to be better informed; developing design appreciation and interpersonal skills is a step in the right direction. The best design managers may come from design courses. □ New technology and disposable income have combined to provide opportunities for new members of our profession to work internationally. Many design groups are no longer confined to the boundaries of their own country, and the opportunity to broaden experiences is real. This suggests the need for foreign language skills and knowledge of and experience with other cultures. □ International exposure of student work brings peer recognition and job opportunities. This book provides professional designers around the world with insight into the new generation's work. Comparing the best work on a global basis prompts us to raise our standards. When my first project was published in a Graphis annual, I knew that something I had produced had met the standards of quality of my peers. No longer do student designers have to wait for this affirmation. This book is long overdue. ■

KEN CATO IS CHAIRMAN OF CATO DESIGN INC. AND A FREQUENT SPEAKER AT ART COLLEGES. HIS AWARD-WINNING WORK HAS BEEN PUBLISHED IN EVERY MAJOR GRAPHIC ARTS MAGAZINE. CATO'S COMMITMENT TO THE GROWTH OF YOUNG DESIGN PROFESSIONALS LED TO THE CREATION OF THE IDEAS STUDENT CONFERENCE. HE SERVES ON ADVISORY BOARDS FOR A NUMBER OF EDUCATIONAL INSTITUTIONS. IN 1995 CATO WAS AWARDED THE FIRST HONORARY DOCTORATE IN DESIGN FROM SWINBURNE UNIVERSITY, AUSTRALIA.

Die Vermittlung der Fähigkeit, Neuland zu erforschen VON KEN CATO

Ein Designkurs ist der erste Schritt einer endlosen Reise. Es ist eine Lernerfahrung, die denen, die sich auf diese Reise begeben, viel Freude, Frustration und Vergnügen bereitet, letzteres hoffentlich auch jenen, die mit den Ergebnissen in Berührung kommen. □ «Ich verbringe nie die ganze Zeit mit praktischer Arbeit.» Ich weiss nicht mehr, wer das gesagt hat, aber dieser Ausspruch könnte von mir und vielen anderen Kollegen stammen, die ständig auf der Suche nach einer besseren Ausdrucksform oder Lösung sind, gleichgültig, an was für einem Projekt sie gerade arbeiten. Unsere Arbeit ist ein ununterbrochener Lernprozess. Es gibt viele begabte und intuitive Leute, die Autodidakten sind und heute zu den Top-Designern zählen, aber die meisten von uns haben eine Hochschule oder Designfachschule besucht. □ Neue Technologien und neue Medien haben unsere Arbeitsweise verändert, und sie bieten uns ganz neue Möglichkeiten. Ein grosser Teil neuer Aufträge ist weitgehend von der Technologie und den damit verbundenen Arbeitsprozessen beeinflusst. Der Computerfaktor hat viele etablierte Designfirmen gezwungen, ihre Struktur und Arbeitsweise zu überdenken. Der ganze Beruf hat sich verändert. Aber auch die Kunden und ihr Verhältnis zum Design haben sich verändert. In Wirtschaftskreisen begreift man allmählich, welchen strategischen und kommunikativen Wert Design hat und wie gross der Einfluss auf den wirtschaftlichen Erfolg eines Unternehmens sein kann. □ Angesichts dieser beiden Phänomene stellt sich die Frage, welche Art von Ausbildung die Universitäten und Designschulen bieten müssen. Ein fein abgestimmtes Mass an verschiedenen Eigenschaften würde den idealen Studienabgänger ausmachen: Er wäre begierig, neue Denkmodelle und wegbereitende neue Lösungen zu erforschen. Hinzu kämen Sensibilität, Stil und ästhetische Intuition sowie die Begabung zu kommunizieren und Auftraggeber zu überzeugen, dass gutes Design gute Kommunikation bedeutet. □ Wir müssen sorgfältig prüfen, wen wir mit den Designkursen ansprechen möchten. Oft belegen Studenten Designkurse, weil sie weder für Naturwissenschaften noch für Medizin oder Wirtschaftswissenschaften geeignet scheinen, dagegen aber eine zeichnerische Begabung haben. Talent allein reicht allerdings nicht. Wir wissen, dass weniger Begabte oft einfach härter arbeiten und das mit gutem Erfolg. In jedem Fall sollte man aber die richtigen jungen Leute anziehen;

danach kann man über die vielen Möglichkeiten sprechen, die unser Beruf bietet. □ Ich war immer überzeugt, dass ein möglichst breiter Bereich von Themen und handwerklichen Techniken im Grundkursus gelehrt werden sollten, um dem Studenten das Selbstvertrauen zu geben, das er braucht, um allen Anforderungen gewachsen zu sein und neue Wege zu gehen. In dieser Gleichung gibt es allerdings eine Unbekannte: die Persönlichkeit des Studenten. Bei Design geht es nicht darum, etwas auf eine bestimmte Art zu machen. Bei einem Projekt sind vielleicht mehrere Lösungen möglich, aber das Besondere ist schliesslich die individuelle Vision des Designers. □ Es hat sehr lange gedauert, bis unsere Branche daran dachte, ihren Nachwuchs zu fördern. Wir müssen auch weiterhin die Universitäten und Design-Fachschulen ermutigen, den Studenten ausreichend Gelegenheit zu geben, mit erfahrenen Praktikern in Berührung zu kommen. Je breiter das Spektrum der Praktiker ist, desto breiter wird der Horizont der jungen Leute werden. Es gibt verschiedene Tagungen wie z.B. die Icograda Conference in London und die IDEAS Students Design Conference in Melbourne, wo Studenten jedes Jahr die Möglichkeit haben, sich mit den ganz unterschiedlichen Arbeiten der Praktiker auseinanderzusetzen. □ Allgemein sind die Gelegenheiten der Studenten, mit internationalen Designern in Berührung zu kommen, auf wenige Stunden beschränkt. Dabei sind frische Einflüsse ungeheuer wichtig. Weniger Unterrichtsstunden und der Druck, ein viel grösseres Lernprogramm in reduzierter Zeit zu bewältigen, haben zu gewissen Zwängen geführt, die wenig erfreulich sind. Ich bin mir durchaus bewusst, wie wichtig die technologische Entwicklung und die damit verbundenen neuen Möglichkeiten sind, aber trotzdem müssen die Grundlagen unseres Berufes vermittelt werden. Wir wollen den Studenten eine praxisnahe handwerkliche und intellektuelle Ausbildung geben, bzw. die Anlagen des Einzelnen fördern. Die zukünftigen Gestalter müssen lernen, nicht nur als Teil eines Designteams zu arbeiten, sondern als Teil eines Netzwerkes von Kunden und anderen Experten wie Architekten, Innenarchitekten, Mode-Designern usw. □ Wir sollten allerdings nicht nur an Designer, sondern auch an jene denken, die mit Design zu tun haben. Ein sicherer Weg, zu besserer Designarbeit zu gelangen, ist die Ausbildung jener, die später die Auftraggeber sein werden. Aus den Designkursen könnten

KEN CATO IST CHAIRMAN VON CATO DESIGN INC. UND HÄUFIGER REFERENT AN DESIGN-SCHULEN UND BEI FACHSEMINAREN. SEINE ARBEITEN WURDEN INTERNATIONAL AUSGEZEICHNET. KEN CATOS ENGAGEMENT IN DER FÖRDERUNG JUNGER DESIGNER FÜHRTE ZUR IDEAS STUDENTS CONFERENCE. ER IST MITGLIED VERSCHIEDENER BEIRÄTE FÜR EINE GANZE ANZAHL VON DESIGNSCHULEN UND -VERBÄNDEN. 1995 VERLIEH DIE SWINBURNE UNIVERSITY, AUSTRALIEN, KEN CATO DEN ERSTEN EHRENDOKTOR IN DESIGN.

hervorragende Design-Manager hervorgehen. Der Bedarf an Design-Managern in den Unternehmen ist offenkundig. Wir alle möchten, dass unsere Auftraggeber besser informiert sind; wenn es gelingt, Wissen und Urteilsvermögen in dieser Richtung zu fördern, sind wir auf dem richtigen Weg. □ Die neue Technologie und die nötigen finanziellen Mittel haben es einigen von uns ermöglicht, auf internationaler Basis zu arbeiten. Viele Designfirmen sind nicht mehr an die Grenzen ihres Landes gebunden, und die Chancen, Erfahrungen auf breiter Basis zu sammeln, sind vorhanden. Das heisst, dass weitere Fähigkeiten wie Fremdsprachenkenntnisse und Erfahrung mit anderen Kulturen nützlich sein werden. □ Auf dem Arbeitsmarkt wird mehr denn je in allen Gewässern gefischt. Die Ausbildung ist für die Einstellung eines Graphikers selten ausschlaggebend. Die wichtigste Voraussetzung ist ganz allein die Qualität der Arbeit, die er vorzeigen kann. In unserem Beruf ist sie sichtbar. Also sollte man die Arbeit für sich selbst sprechen lassen. □ Wenn die Arbeit von Studenten einem internationalen Publikum vorgestellt wird, dann bringt das Anerkennung von Fachleuten und Chancen auf dem Arbeitsmarkt. Der vorliegende Band gewährt den gestandenen Designern Einblick in die Arbeit der neuen Generation. Dieser internationale Vergleich wird dazu beitragen, die Qualitätsansprüche zu heben. Als zum ersten Mal eine Arbeit von mir im Graphis (Design) Annual erschien, bedeutete das für mich, dass etwas, das ich gemacht hatte, gut genug war, um im internationalen Vergleich zu bestehen. Diese Chance wurde hier den Studenten gegeben. Das Buch war längst fällig. ∎

Repousser toujours plus loin les limites de l'exploration PAR KEN CATO

Commencer une formation de design est le début d'un long parcours. Une histoire sans fin en qulque sorte. C'est un processus d'apprentissage intense qui apporte son lot de joies, de frustrations, de plaisirs à ceux qui osent s'aventurer dans une telle voie. □ «Je ne passe pas tout mon temps à travailler concrètement». Je ne sais plus qui a dit cela, mais cela s'applique certainement à mon cas et à beaucoup de mes collègues designers, qui sont constamment à la recherche d'une nouvelle idée, d'une expression ou d'une solution originale, quelle que soit la nature du projet qui les occupe. C'est un processus d'auto-éducation permanent. Un certain nombre de personnes intuitives et particulièrement douées ont réussi à se propulser au sommet de notre profession en autodidactes, sans avoir fréquenté une école de design. Cependant, la majorité d'entre nous a suivi une formation académique. □ Les nouveaux média et technologies sont en train de changer notre manière de travailler et nous ouvrent de nouveaux horizons. Une bonne partie des mandats fait appel aujourd'hui à la technologie et aux processus novateurs qu'elle introduit. L'apparition de l'ordinateur a obligé de nombreuses agences de design à repenser leurs structures et leur manière de travailler. La profession de designer a changé, mais également la clientèle et sa relation au design. Les milieux économiques commencent à reconnaître l'importance stratégique du design dans la communication et la façon dont celui-ci peut influencer le succès de l'entreprise. □ En tenant compte de cette double évolution, quel genre de professionnels les écoles de design et les universités doivent-elles former? L'étudiant idéal devrait présenter des qualités multiples, combinées en un savant mélange: il serait curieux, toujours prêt à explorer de nouvelles idées, à sortir des sentiers battus, à rechercher des solutions décapantes. Il se distinguerait par son sens inné de la communication, son intuition pour l'esthétique, sa sensibilité et son style. Enfin, il saurait convaincre le client qu'un bon design sert une bonne communication. □ Qui sont les futurs professionnels que nous souhaitons former? Certains étudiants se retrouvent en classe de design parce qu'ils n'étaient pas assez bons en sciences, en médecine ou en économie et qu'ils étaient doués en dessin. Mais le talent seul n'est jamais suffisant. Beaucoup de gens réussissent sans avoir beaucoup de talent, parce qu'ils travaillent plus dur que les autres. Il semble néanmoins logique de vouloir attirer en priorité les bons éléments. Ensuite, les nombreuses possibilités de carrière qu'offre notre profession peuvent être présentées. □ J'ai toujours pensé qu'en enseignant un vaste éventail de matières et en présentant diverses techniques dès le début d'un cours, les designers disposeraient du bagage nécessaire pour explorer de nouvelles solutions et relever toutes sortes de défis. Le design ne se réduit pas à une manière de procéder, de multiples approches

KEN CATO EST PRÉSIDENT DE CATO DESIGN INC. DANS LE CADRE DE SES ACTIVITÉS, IL DONNE RÉGULIÈREMENT DES CONFÉRENCES DANS LES ÉCOLES D'ART DU MONDE ENTIER AINSI QU'À L'OCCASION DE SÉMINAIRES PROFESSIONNELS. SON ENGAGEMENT ENVERS LES JEUNES GRAPHISTES A DÉBOUCHÉ SUR L'IDEAS STUDENT CONFERENCE. EN 1995, LA SWINBURNE UNIVERSITY, AUSTRALIE, LUI A DÉCERNÉ LE PREMIER TITRE DE DOCTEUR HONORIS CAUSA ÈS ARTS GRAPHIQUES.

sont possibles. Ce qui distingue en fait un projet d'un autre, c'est la vision personnelle du designer. □ Il s'agit également d'encourager les universités et les écoles à instaurer un dialogue permanent entre les étudiants et les professionnels de la branche. Plus la diversité des contacts sera grande, plus les designers auront l'occasion d'élargir leur horizon. Il existe à l'heure actuelle différentes conférences, comme l'Icograda Conference à Londres et l'IDEAS Student Design Conference à Melbourne, qui offrent chaque année aux étudiants la possibilité de se confronter à la grande variété de styles pratiqués par les designers du monde entier. □ En général, les étudiants ont rarement la chance d'être en contact avec des designers internationaux, c'est pourquoi il est crucial d'encourager ces contacts. La réduction des heures de cours et l'obligation d'enseigner toujours plus de matières dans un temps limité ont forcé les écoles à effectuer des choix pas toujours très heureux. Même si je suis conscient de l'importance des nouvelles possibilités offertes par la technologie, j'estime qu'il faut continuer à enseigner les bases du métier. Nous voulons développer les aptitudes pratiques des étudiants au même titre que leur créativité. Nos futurs designers doivent apprendre à travailler en équipe, être capables de s'intégrer dans un vaste réseau de clients, d'architectes, d'architectes d'intérieur, de dessinateurs de mode, etc. □ Je pense qu'il est également important de cultiver l'intérêt du public pour le design, de le sensibiliser à notre profession. Si l'on désire élever le niveau de qualité du design, il convient d'«éduquer» les clients potentiels. Il est impératif d'avoir des personnes compétentes en matière de design au sein de chaque entreprise. Nous voulons tous que nos clients soient mieux informés. Si nous développons leur capacité à évaluer et à apprécier le travail bien fait, nous allons dans la bonne direction. □ Les nouvelles technologies et les moyens financiers à disposition ont permis à certains membres de notre corporation de travailler sur le plan international. L'activité de nombreuses agences de design ne se limite pas aux frontières d'un pays. Les possibilités de diversifier les expériences sont réelles, ce qui signifie que la connaissance d'autres langues et d'autres cultures peut être un atout majeur. □ Les perspectives professionnelles sont plus vastes que jamais. Il est rare que les titres académiques seuls permettent aux designers d'obtenir un travail. Le critère essentiel est et reste toujours la qualité des travaux, qualité qui se laisse juger par le seul regard. Laissons donc le travail parler par lui-même. □ Lorsque les travaux des étudiants peuvent – comme c'est le cas dans cet ouvrage – être présentés à un public international, il en résulte une reconnaissance professionnelle qui peut ouvrir certaines perspectives d'emploi. Ce livre permettra aux professionnels du monde entier de prendre la mesure du talent de la nouvelle génération. Je me souviens que lorsque mon premier projet fut publié dans le Graphis Annual, j'ai soudain réalisé qu'une de mes réalisations était d'un niveau de qualité suffisant pour figurer à côté d'autres travaux de professionnels. Voilà un livre que j'attendais depuis longtemps et qui donne enfin une chance réelle aux étudiants. ■

Conduits for a Changing Profession BY CHRIS HILL

PORTRAIT BY TRELEVEN PHOTOGRAPHY

Design education is receiving more attention than ever before–attention, in my view, that is long overdue. However, the ongoing debate over the role that concerned parties should play in shaping design education often overlooks the fact that the profession is in the midst of unprecedented rapid change. The question is, how do we provide students with the flexibility to adapt to a constantly evolving environment? □ We should first examine the primary source of this evolution in the design profession: modern technology. The growth of the computer industry has produced an array of media unforseeable even a few years ago. Consider that the average design student takes four or five years to complete a university-level degree, then think about the technological changes that have recently taken place in that same amount of time. Multimedia, interactive CD-ROM, the Internet–all of these were unheard of a few years ago. A modern design program must produce professionals who can adapt quickly to these and other innovations that are certain to follow. □ It will always be true that the core of a good design program is a solid curriculum which provides students with a sure understanding of typography, layout, color, and form–the building blocks of design. Equally important is the ability to respond with skill and imagination to the shifting needs of a marketplace increasingly dominated by high technology. A curriculum that is too rigid or too bound to one design philosophy serves neither itself nor its students. It is an unfortunate that many colleges and universities lack the means to make rapid adjustments to their programs even if they wish to. For instance, freshmen who begin a design program in a state-of-the-art computer graphics lab all too often find themselves working as seniors in a room full of technological antiques. If a college or university lacks the funds for proper upgrades or the determination to keep its program current, its students will be unprepared to meet the demands of the profession. □ Having recognized the enormous impact of modern technology on the design field, we must now point out that creative flexibility depends less on computer expertise than on the development of strong conceptual thinking and problem solving skills. Computer expertise supplies the tools now required by the work environ-

ment, but the ability to generate concepts and ideas remains key to a good design education. Programs too often favor the instantaneous glitz of a computer-generated "look," or focus exclusively on the latest trends in cutting-edge style. The problem is that changes in graphic style are not only continual, but also unpredictable. Colleges and universities that allow their programs to emphasize style over substance ignore this reality at their own risk. □ The growth of independent conceptual thinking depends on a broad understanding of the history of graphic design. Educational programs should incorporate a comprehensive survey of design not only to communicate the historical influences that continue to have an impact on the profession today, but also to familiarize students with groundbreaking design movements from around the world. This should involve much more than the "copycat" principle by which students simply reinterpret elements from influential work, moving each time further and further from the original inspiration that gave the work its force in the first place. Instead, design education should encourage students to probe the creative process involved in developing a great concept and bringing it to realization. This requires a solid grasp of the historical context. □ Another vital avenue for approaching the creative process is provided by design professionals themselves. Many university programs already draw on designers from the local community to supplement the efforts of their full-time instructors. Not only do these working professionals serve as an essential conduit for innovations going on in the marketplace, but they represent an important source of inspiration available to explain the inner workings—from false starts to sudden revelations—behind the development of an idea. □ To educators and students the prospect of an international student design competition is very exciting. While professionals have a sizable number of award shows and annuals jockeying for their work, opportunities for students to compete on an expanded stage are rare. This book allows students not only to measure themselves against other students from around the world, but also to evaluate other programs based on the strength of their entries. Design education will benefit from this new standard of excellence, and the exposure awarded the work of winning students should lead to career opportunities that would be otherwise less accessible to them. This coalescing of talents and influences will have a pos-

CHRIS HILL IS PRESIDENT AND CREATIVE DIRECTOR OF HILL/A MARKETING DESIGN GROUP, INC., IN HOUSTON, TEXAS. HIS MANY CLIENTS INCLUDE COMPAQ COMPUTERS, DORITOS FOODS, PEPSICO, AND SHELL CHEMICAL. HILL'S AWARD-WINNING DESIGNS HAVE BEEN RECOGNIZED BY THE AMERICAN INSTITUTE OF GRAPHIC ARTS, AMERICAN CENTER FOR DESIGN, AND THE ART DIRECTORS CLUB OF NEW YORK.

itive effect on both the education arena and the market. □ As a professional designer, I encourage you to take an active role in design education in your area. Not only does it ensure the vitality of the profession, but it creates mutual excitement crucial to a field undergoing constant change. With the energetic participation of working professionals, college and university programs should be able to avoid the limitations of an overly static approach to design and instead open up opportunities for students to explore and excel in the ever-multiplying aspects of today's creative environment. ■

Eine Berufsausbildung im Wandel VON CHRIS HILL

Der Ausbildung von Designern wird heute grössere Aufmerksamkeit zuteil denn je, was meiner Meinung nach längst überfällig war. Bei der Diskussion über die Rolle, die die verschiedenen Parteien in der Design-Ausbildung zu spielen haben, wird oft übersehen, dass sich der Beruf heute mitten im Umbruch befindet, der viel schneller vor sich geht als erwartet. Die Frage ist deshalb: Wie geben wir den Studenten die nötige Flexibilität, sich diesen rapiden Veränderungen anzupassen? □ Wir sollten uns zuerst mit der Hauptursache für diesen ständigen Wandel in unserem Beruf befassen – der neuen Technologie. Die Computerindustrie hat eine ganze Reihe von neuen Medien geschaffen, die noch vor wenigen Jahren nicht denkbar waren. Nehmen wir einmal den durchschnittlichen Design-Studenten, der 4–5 Jahre braucht, um einen Hochschul– oder gleichwertigen Abschluss zu machen und betrachten dann die technologischen Veränderungen, die in der gleichen Zeit stattgefunden haben. Multimedia. Interaktive CD-ROM. Das Internet. Von all dem hat man vor ein paar Jahren noch nichts gewusst. Eine moderne Design-Ausbildung muss Fachleute hervorbringen, die sich diesen und anderen Innovationen, die ohne Zweifel folgen werden, schnell anpassen können. □ Der Kern einer guten Designausbildung ist zweifellos nach wie vor ein solider Lehrplan, der dem Studenten ein gutes Verständnis von Typographie, Layout, Farbe und Form vermittelt....die Grundsteine des Designs. Genau so wichtig ist heute jedoch die Fähigkeit, sich mit Geschick und Phantasie den wechselnden Bedürfnissen eines Marktes anzupassen, der zunehmend von hochentwickelter Technologie bestimmt wird. Ein Lehrplan, der zu starr ist, zu sehr an eine bestimmte Design-Auffassung gebunden, dient weder dem Institut noch den Studenten. Es ist in diesem Zusammenhang bedauerlich, dass vielen Schulen und Universitäten die Mittel fehlen, ihren Lehrplan den Bedürfnissen schnell anzupassen. □ Studienanfänger, deren Ausbildung mit einem Computer-Graphik-Programm beginnt, finden sich nur allzuoft in einem Raum voller technologischer Antiquitäten wieder. Wenn es an finanziellen Mitteln oder der nötigen Überzeugung fehlt, um die Ausrüstung für einen Lehrgang mit den entsprechenden Upgrades auf dem neusten Stand zu halten, können die Schulen und Universitäten ihre Studenten nicht auf die heutigen Anforderungen ihres Berufes vorbereiten. □ Nachdem der enorme Einfluss der modernen Technologie im Bereich des Designs erwähnt wurde, sei hier klar gesagt, dass kreative Flexibilität weniger von den Computer-Fähigkeiten als von der auf konzeptuelles Denken und Problemlösungen ausgerichteten Ausbildung abhängt. Das Beherrschen des Computers gibt dem Studenten das nötige Werkzeug in die Hand, um im heutigen Arbeitsumfeld zurecht zu kommen, aber die Fähigkeit, Konzepte und Ideen zu entwickeln, ist nach wie vor der Kern einer guten Designausbildung. Nur allzu häufig wird an den Schulen die glatte, schnelle Computergraphik favorisiert bzw. die allerneusten, sogenannten «cutting edge»-Stilrichtungen. Das Problem ist, dass sich der graphische Stil heute nicht nur ständig verändert, sondern auch unberechenbar ist. Schulen, bei denen Stil über Substanz geht, übersehen diese Realität zu ihrem eigenen Nachteil. □ Die Entwicklungsfähigkeit im Bereich des konzeptuellen Denkens hängt von dem Verständnis der Geschichte des Graphik-Designs ab. Ausbildungsprogramme sollten deshalb einen umfassenden Überblick über das gestalterische Schaffen bieten, und zwar nicht nur, um die historischen Einflüsse aufzuzeigen, die auch heute noch eine Rolle spielen, sondern auch, um die Studenten über bahnbrechende Design-Bewegungen in allen Teilen der Welt zu informieren. Das würde heissen, dass viel mehr als das Kopieren alter Meister gefragt ist, bei dem es nur darum geht, sich Schritt für Schritt von der Originalidee zu entfernen, die die eigentliche Stärke der Arbeit ausmachte. Statt dessen sollten die Studenten dazu angehalten

CHRIS HILL IST PRÄSIDENT UND CREATIVE DIRECTOR VON HILL/A MARKETING DESIGN GROUP, INC. IN HOUSTON, TEXAS. ZU SEINEN ZAHLREICHEN KUNDEN GEHÖREN COMPAQ COMPUTERS, DORITOS FOODS, PEPSI CO. UND SHELL CHEMICAL. HILLS ARBEITEN WURDEN MEHRFACH AUSGEZEICHNET, U.A. VOM AIGA, DEM AMERICAN CENTER FOR DESIGN UND DEM ART DIRECTORS CLUB OF NEW YORK.

werden, sich im kreativen Prozess zu üben, der zur Entwicklung und Umsetzung eines hervorragenden Konzeptes führt. Das erfordert ein solides Verständnis des historischen Kontextes. □ Eine andere Voraussetzung, um die Studenten mit dem kreativen Prozess vertraut zu machen, ist der Kontakt mit Design-Praktikern. Viele Universitäten verpflichten bereits Praktiker aus ihrer Region als Gastreferenten zur Unterstützung des Lehrkörpers. Die Studenten profitieren von der praxisnahen Erfahrung der Designer, nicht nur was die mit neusten Entwicklungen in ihrer Branche angeht, sondern auch im Hinblick auf Ratschläge und Anregungen; sie erfahren etwas über das, was hinter der Entwicklung von Ideen steht – von falschen Anfängen bis zu plötzlichen Erleuchtungen. □ Für Lehrer und Studenten ist ein internationaler Studentenwettbewerb eine sehr aufregende Sache. Denn während es für die Praktiker eine ganze Anzahl von Ausstellungen, Preisen und Jahrbüchern gibt, die sich um ihre Arbeiten reissen, sind für Studenten Gelegenheiten, sich einem Wettbewerb in grösserem Rahmen zu stellen, selten. Dieses Forum gibt den Studenten nicht nur die Möglichkeit, sich mit anderen Studenten aus aller Welt zu messen, sondern sie können auch die anderen Schulen anhand der Qualität der Studentenarbeiten einschätzen. Von diesem Vergleich wird auch die Designausbildung im allgemeinen profitieren. Hinzu kommt, dass sich den Studenten durch die Veröffentlichung ihrer Arbeit berufliche Möglichkeiten eröffnen könnten, die sich sonst kaum ergeben hätten. Diese Verbindung von Talent und Einfluss wird im Bereich der Schulen wie auch für den Arbeitsmarkt einen positiven Effekt haben. □ Als Designer möchte ich meine Kollegen auffordern, eine aktive Rolle in der Design-Ausbildung zu übernehmen. Damit wird nicht nur die Dynamik in unserer Branche gefördert, sondern auch eine gegenseitige Inspiration, die angesichts der ständigen Veränderungen ungeheuer wichtig ist. Die Einbeziehung von Fachleuten aus der Berufspraxis sollte ein zu starres Lehrprogramm im Designbereich an den Ausbildungsstätten verhindern und statt dessen den Studenten die Möglichkeit geben, sich mit den heute unendlich scheinenden Aspekten des kreativen Berufes vertraut zu machen und sich hier zu bewähren. ∎

Une profession en mutation PAR CHRIS HILL

On ne s'est jamais autant interrogé sur la formation des graphistes qu'aujourd'hui et je serais tenté de dire qu'il était temps. Or le débat sur le rôle que doivent jouer les diverses parties prenantes à cette formation ignore souvent le fait que la profession traverse actuellement une mutation d'une rapidité sans précédent. Comment, dans ces conditions, donner aux étudiants la souplesse leur permettant de s'adapter à une situation qui ne cesse d'évoluer? Telle est bien la question. □ Intéressons-nous d'abord à ce qui est la cause principale des incessants changements que connaît notre profession: la technologie. L'industrie informatique a donné le jour à toute une série de nouveaux médias que nul n'aurait encore osé imaginer voilà quelques années. Prenons le cas de l'étudiant en arts graphiques type, qui mettra quatre ou cinq ans pour décrocher un diplôme universitaire ou un titre jugé équivalent, et considérons les changements technologiques intervenus durant ce laps de temps. Multimédia. CD-ROM interactif. Internet. Toutes choses parfaitement inconnues il y a quelques années. Une formation moderne doit donc permettre l'éclosion de spécialistes capables de s'adapter rapidement à ces innovations ainsi qu'à celles dont elles seront sans aucun doute suivies. □ Une bonne formation de graphiste s'articulera toujours autour d'un cursus bien bâti, donnant à l'étudiant un sens affirmé de la typographie, de la mise en page, de la couleur et de la forme, lesquelles constituent les bases de son métier. Mais elle doit aussi, et plus que jamais, développer en lui l'aptitude à répondre avec savoir-faire et imagination aux besoins changeants d'un marché de plus en plus fortement dominé par la haute technologie. Un cursus par trop rigide, par trop attaché à une conception particulariste des arts graphiques ne profiterait ni à l'établissement qui donne la formation ni à ceux et à celles qui la reçoivent. Notons à ce propos, à regret, que beaucoup d'écoles et d'universités ne disposent malheureusement pas des fonds qui leur permettraient d'ajuster rapidement leur cursus à l'évolution des besoins. □ Trop souvent l'étudiant de première année, dont la formation commence par un programme graphique sur ordinateur, se trouve condamné à des équipements complètement vétustes. Comment des établissements n'ayant ni les moyens financiers ni

CHRIS HILL EST PRÉSIDENT ET DIRECTEUR DE CRÉATION DU HILL/A MARKETING DESIGN GROUP INC. À HOUSTON, TEXAS. PARMIS SES NOMBREUX CLIENTS FIGURENT COMPAQ COMPUTERS, DORITOS FOODS, PEPSI CO. ET SHELL CHEMICAL. HILL S'EST VU DÉCERNER PLUSIEURS PRIX POUR SES TRAVAUX, ENTRE AUTRES PAR L'AIGA, L'AMERICAN CENTER FOR DESIGN ET LE ART DIRECTORS CLUB DE NEW YORK.

la volonté pédagogique de remettre constamment à niveau leurs outils didactiques pourraient-ils préparer leurs étudiants aux exigences actuelles du métier? □ Après avoir évoqué la technologie et l'énorme impact qu'elle a aujourd'hui sur le design, il est temps de préciser que la souplesse et la créativité dépendent moins de la maîtrise de l'ordinateur que d'un enseignement sachant développer chez l'étudiant la faculté de conceptualiser sa pensée et de trouver des solutions pratiques aux problèmes qui lui sont posés. La maîtrise de l'ordinateur lui donne les outils dont il a besoin dans l'environnement professionnel actuel, mais la capacité à faire naître des concepts et des idées reste la pierre angulaire de toute bonne formation de graphiste. L'enseignement a trop souvent tendance à privilégier le caractère instantané, lisse et poli de la création d'images assistée par ordinateur et à insister plus que de raison sur ce que les modes véhiculent de plus éphémère. Le problème, c'est que les styles changent constamment, et de façon imprévisible. Les établissements qui, plaçant le style au-dessus de la substance, méconnaissent cette réalité risquent de le regretter un jour. □ Le développement des facultés de conceptualisation de l'étudiant passe par la connaissance de l'histoire des arts graphiques. Son intégration aux programmes d'enseignement aurait pour effet de sensibiliser l'étudiant aux influences historiques qui perdurent jusqu'à nos jours et de le familiariser avec les grands mouvements qui, partant de toutes les parties du monde, révolutionnent périodiquement la création graphique. Dans la mesure où la copie n'est jamais qu'une réplique affadie de l'original, il ne s'agit toutefois pas de transformer l'étudiant en copiste des anciens maîtres, mais, bien au contraire, de roder en lui le processus de création conduisant à développer et à réaliser des concepts de qualité. Et cela suppose de sa part une bonne connaissance du contexte historique. □ Le contact avec des graphistes pratiquant déjà le métier est un autre moyen de familiariser l'étudiant avec ce processus de création. Beaucoup d'universités font déjà appel à des graphistes locaux pour compléter les cours de leur propre corps enseignant. L'expérience pratique de ces professionnels, leurs conseils, leurs suggestions sont pour les étudiants d'un profit allant bien au-delà des dernières nouveautés et tendances du métier. Ils découvrent à leur contact la façon dont naissent les idées, des faux départs à la soudaine illumination. □ Un concours est toujours, pour les étudiants comme pour les enseignants, une expérience très stimulante. Alors qu'il existe pour les professionnels toute une série d'expositions, de prix et de publications annuelles, pour lesquels on s'arrache leurs travaux, les étudiants ont rarement l'occasion de se présenter à un concours jouissant de quelque notoriété. Pour eux, c'est donc là l'occasion de se mesurer à des étudiants du monde entier et de comparer les mérites respectifs des écoles dont émanent les travaux exposés. La formation des graphistes ne peut qu'y gagner. La publication des travaux peut en outre leur ouvrir des portes pour l'avenir, et il est permis de penser que cette initiative conjuguant talent et notoriété aura un effet bénéfique au niveau des écoles ainsi que du marché de l'emploi. □ Etant moi-même graphiste, j'encourage mes collègues à prendre dans leur communauté une part active à la formation des graphistes. Cela ne peut que dynamiser notre branche et créer une émulation d'autant plus nécessaire que notre profession va de mutation en mutation. Souhaitons qu'en donnant la parole à des praticiens, l'enseignement des arts graphiques parvienne à éviter certaines pesanteurs et rigidités et conduise, au contraire, les étudiants à explorer les mille et une facettes de leur futur métier et à épanouir leur talent. ■

Are We There Yet? BY STEVEN SKOV HOLT

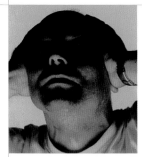

NOTES TOWARD A NEW AGENDA FOR DESIGN CONSCIOUSNESS □ Since design schools are, by principle, about the exploration and creation of what is not yet necessarily manifest, I have a question: What might designers, students, and institutions do to expand design consciousness—how might we raise awareness in order to see successful explorations and creations manifest themselves in the productions of tomorrow? □ Several possibilities come to mind. For example: **Design might define a presence on TV, in cinema and on the Internet.** In the 1970s, design was covered in specialized trade magazines; in the 1980s, design expanded to a much larger group of consumer magazines and newspapers; in the 1990s, the action will center around getting design—its iterative, magical process, its creative characters, its narrative content—on-screen for an exponentially larger audience. When we can see and hear "design news" on CNN, AOL, MTV—when we can tune into The Design Channel or the still-to-be-conceived "Design Network," then we will know design has arrived. □ **Design might be taught at our country's best universities.** We live amidst more images and products than ever before, yet the highest seats of learning have essentially nothing to do with design. When industrial design, graphic design, illustration and photography are taught at Harvard—at the graduate level—then we will know design has arrived. □ **Design students might develop an enhanced anthropological awareness.** At CCAC in San Francisco, we analyze the phenomenon of Post-Market Product Alteration. The goal of PMPA studies is to get deeper inside the mindset of consumers by looking at how people customize their own products. When designers and marketers create powerful empathy with users by jointly pursuing explorations into subject matter such as painted boom-boxes, magnet-plastered refrigerators, and Post-it-covered computer bezels, then we will know design has arrived. □ **Design programs might address the profound disconnection between the skill sets with which students graduate, and those employers want them to have.** Consider team-based problem solving, for example. Due to the scale, scope and schedule of projects at many agencies, it simply isn't possible for one person to know it all. When form follows collaboration—when team-based research, creativity, decision-making and learning are part of each program's core values—then we will know design has arrived. □ **Design might be taught in elementary schools—as well as in MBA programs.** Then we might have children who understand the role that design plays in consumerism, as well as decision-makers who strategically use design for competitive market advantage. When product-based issues of form, function and meaning can be explained and comprehended by someone in the corner candy store as well as in the corner office—when the profession approximates the gender and ethnic proportions of the larger population—then we will know design has arrived. □ **Design educators might tune in to areas of educational reform.** Peggy McIntosh, Director of Wellesley College's Center for Research on Women, has argued for ways of learning that go beyond a win/lose mentality. We need to emphasize team-based collaboration more than individual competition. When we have design curricula that create learning environments with the feeling of familial support rather than of tournaments with one winner, then we will know design has arrived. □ **Design educators might utilize "history" to connect ideas, projects and the development of a student's own philosophy of design.** At CCAC, we have brought our resident design historian, Barry Katz, into the studio to underline the essential connection of history and material-culture study to the creative process. When we can get beyond thinking of design history as a "greatest hits parade" with no connection to the creative process, then we will know that design has arrived. □ **Design programs might get rid of tenure.** We could invest in local or national "teaching treasures" by placing them at one of the great state universities—especially since most of the great state universities (like the Ivy League schools) are without design programs. What better catalyst for a nascent program than to have a tribal design elder serve at the core as its inspiration? The rest of the existing faculty might be on a "prove it or lose it" basis. That's today's reality anyway. Knowledge-centered workers (designers and teachers, for example) are finding that they do one job on Mondays, work for a different company on Tuesday and Wednesday afternoons, do another job on Tuesday, Wednesday and Thursday mornings, and have a fourth employer on Fridays. When we have educational hiring organized along the fragmented lines of this new information economy, then we will know that design—and design education—has arrived. □ Designers—and especially design students—might

STEVEN SKOV HOLT IS BOTH VISIONARY AND STRATEGIC DIRECTOR OF FROGDESIGN, SUNNYVALE, CALIFORNIA, AND CHAIR OF THE INDUSTRIAL DESIGN PROGRAM, CALIFORNIA COLLEGE OF ARTS AND CRAFTS (CCAC) SAN FRANCISCO, CALIFORNIA.

creatively respond to the mental challenge of our time—hyperinformation. ☐ In our global economy of information, image and product overload, it is clear that hardware and software will become "softer" and more individualized. Happily, we can see that customizable, flexible, foldable, huggable, multiple-materialed, rubbable, and wearable technology that sometimes even develops a decent patina from use is showing up in the pages of this very Graphis book. This reflects not just the development of a new industry, style and materiality, but the emergence of the most aware generation of designers ever. When this emergent "X" generation takes the reins—and I suspect it will be not a moment too soon—then we will know that design has truly arrived. And we will know, with equal certainty, that it's already time to reinvent visual literacy yet again. ■

Sind wir schon soweit? VON STEVEN SKOV HOLT

NOTIZEN FÜR EINEN PLAN ZUR FÖRDERUNG DES DESIGN-BEWUSSTSEINS ☐ Da Designschulen sich im Prinzip mit der Untersuchung und Herstellung von etwas befassen, das nicht unbedingt für jedermann offenkundig ist, stellt sich die Frage, was wir als Designer, Studenten und Schulen tun könnten, um das Design-Bewusstsein zu fördern – damit sich erfolgreiche Ergebnisse der heutigen Designausbildung in den Produktionen von morgen niederschlagen. ☐ Mir kommen dabei verschiedene Möglichkeiten in den Sinn. Zum Beispiel: **Design könnte im Fernsehen, im Kino und im Internet einen Platz einnehmen.** In den 70er Jahren befassten sich Fachzeitschriften mit Design; in den 80er Jahren wurde das Thema auch von Publikumszeitschriften und Zeitungen aufgegriffen; in den 90er Jahren wird es darum gehen, Design für ein noch grösseres Publikum auf den Bildschirm zu bringen – den Arbeitsprozess, die Kreativen und die erzählerische Qualität des Designs. Wenn wir «Design News» auf CNN, AOL, MTV sehen und hören können – wenn wir den Design-Kanal einschalten können oder das noch zu planende «Design Network», dann werden wir wissen, dass Design am Ziel ist. ☐ **Design könnte an den besten Hochschulen unterrichtet werden.** Wir leben umgeben von mehr Bildern und mehr Produkten denn je zuvor, und doch gibt es an den wichtigsten Universitäten keinen Lehrstuhl für Design. Wenn Industrie-Design, Graphik-Design, Illustration und Photographie an der Harvard Universität gelehrt werden – dann werden wir wissen, dass Design am Ziel ist. ☐ **Design-Studenten könnten sich intensiver mit dem Verhalten und den Bedürfnissen der Menschen befassen.** Am California College of Arts and Crafts in San Francisco untersuchen wir das Phänomen der nachträglichen Bearbeitung von Produkten durch die Verbraucher, die sogenannte «Post-Market Product Alteration». Ziel dieser Untersuchungen ist, tiefer in die Verhaltensweisen der Verbraucher einzudringen, indem wir beobachten, wie sie die Produkte ihren Bedürfnissen anpassen. Wenn Designer und Hersteller gemeinsam mehr Einfühlungsvermögen in dieser Hinsicht entwickeln, indem sie Dinge wie bemalte tragbare Radios, mit Magneten gepflasterte Eisschränke und mit Zetteln übersäte Computerrahmen unter die Lupe nehmen – dann werden wir wissen, dass Design am Ziel ist. ☐ **Die Design-Studiengänge könnten sich mit der Diskrepanz zwischen dem Können der Schulabgänger und den Erwartungen und Anforderungen ihrer zukünftigen Arbeitgeber befassen.** Man denke an die Lösung von Aufgaben innerhalb eines Teams. Angesichts des Umfangs und Terminplans vieler gegenwärtiger Projekte von frogdesign, ist es für eine einzelne Person schlicht unmöglich, alles zu wissen. Wenn die «Form der Zusammenarbeit folgt» – wenn Untersuchungen, Kreativität, Entscheidungen und Lernen im Team zum Kern eines jeden Studienprogramms gehören – dann werden wir wissen, dass Design am Ziel ist. ☐ **Design könnte auch an den Grundschulen und an Wirtschaftshochschulen unterrichtet werden.** Dann könnten bereits Kinder verstehen, welche Rolle Design für den Konsum spielt, wie auch die Entscheidungsträger, die Design als strategischen Marktvorteil gegenüber der Konkurrenz nutzen. Wenn produktbezogene Fragen wie Form, Funktion und Bedeutung von jedermann erklärt und verstanden werden können – wenn unser Beruf breiten Kreisen der Bevölkerung vertraut ist, dann werden wir wissen, dass Design am Ziel ist. ☐ **Design-Professoren könnten sich mit einer Studienreform befassen.** Peggy Mcintosh, Direktorin des Forschungszentrums für Frauen am Wellesley College setzt sich für Lehrmethoden ein, die nichts mit der Gewinner/Verlierer-Mentalität zu tun haben. Wir müssen die Zusammenarbeit im Team mehr fördern statt individuelles

STEVEN SKOV HOLT IST DIREKTOR FÜR UNTERNEHMENSSTRATEGIE UND KREATIVE PLANUNG VON FROGDESIGN, SUNNYVALE, KALIFORNIEN, UND INHABER EINES LEHRSTUHLS FÜR INDUSTRIE-DESIGN AM CALIFORNIA COLLEGE OF ARTS AND CRAFTS VON SAN FRANCISCO (CCAC).

Konkurrenzverhalten. Wenn in den Design-Studiengängen das Lernen von einem Gefühl familiärer Unterstützung geprägt ist statt von einem Wettbewerb mit nur einem Gewinner, dann werden wir wissen, dass Design am Ziel ist. □ **Design-Professoren könnten die Design-Geschichte nutzen, um Ideen, Projekte und die Entwicklung einer eigenen Designauffassung beim Studenten in einen Zusammenhang zu bringen.** Am CCAC haben wir unseren Experten für Design-Geschichte, Barry Katz, ins Atelier geholt, damit er die Studenten über die grundsätzlichen Zusammenhänge zwischen Geschichte, dem Studium des Materials und der Kultur und dem kreativen Prozess aufklärt. Wenn wir es schaffen, in der Geschichte des Designs mehr zu sehen als eine Hit-Parade ohne Einfluss auf den kreativen Prozess, dann werden wir wissen, dass Design am Ziel ist. □ **Design-Studienprogramme könnten von beamteten Lehrern befreit werden.** Wir könnten in regionale oder nationale hochbegabte Design-Pädagogen investieren, indem wir sie an den grossen Universitäten unterrichten lassen – zumal die meisten der grossen Universitäten (wie die Eliteuniversäten der USA) noch keine Design-Studienprogramme anbieten. Was wäre ein besserer Katalysator für ein junges Fach als einer der Stammesältesten an einem Ort, wo er am wirkungsvollsten sein kann. □ Die anderen 95% des Lehrkörpers könnten auf der Basis einer Bewährungsprobe eingestellt werden. Das entspricht ohnehin den heutigen Realitäten. Arbeitskräfte, die ihr Wissen einsetzen (wie z.B. Designer und Lehrer), arbeiten immer öfter für verschiedene Arbeitgeber bzw. an verschiedenen Aufgaben. Wenn wir auch im Unterrichtsbereich entsprechend dieser sporadischen Einsätze verfahren, dann werden wir sicher sein können, dass Design – und Design-Ausbildung – am Ziel sind. □ Designer – und besonders Design-Studenten – könnten auf die geistige Herausforderung unserer Zeit, die Hyper-Information, kreativ reagieren. □ In unserer globalen wirtschaftlichen Situation mit einer Überlastung durch Information, Bilder und Produkte ist es klar, dass Hardware und Software «softer», mehr auf den Einzelnen abgestimmt sein müssen. Erfreulicherweise taucht auf den Seiten des vorliegenden Bandes jene anpassungsfähige, flexible, biegsame, anschmiegsame, liebenswerte, ausdauernde Technologie auf, die manchmal sogar ein wenig Patina vom häufigen Gebrauch angesetzt hat. Das widerspiegelt nicht nur die Entwicklung einer neuen Industrie, eines neuen Stils und einer neuen Materialität, sondern auch das Auftauchen der aufgewecktesten Generation von Designern, die es je gab. Wenn diese neue Generation X die Zügel in die Hand nimmt – und ich vermute, das wird keine Minute zu früh geschehen –, dann werden wir wissen, dass Design wirklich am Ziel ist. Und wir werden mit der gleichen Gewissheit sagen können, dass es bereits wieder an der Zeit ist, die visuelle Kultur neu zu erfinden. ∎

Touchons-nous au but ? PAR STEVEN SKOV HOLT

NOTES ET RÉFLEXIONS SUR L'ÉVOLUTION DU DESIGN □ L'objectif premier des écoles de design étant de créer et d'explorer ce qui n'est pas forcément manifeste, la question se pose de savoir ce que nous, designers, étudiants et écoles pouvons mettre en œuvre pour favoriser une nouvelle prise de conscience du design. De quels moyens disposons-nous pour que les évolutions réjouissantes de notre branche profitent aux productions de demain? □ Diverses possibilités viennent à l'esprit. En voici quelques-unes: **Le design pourrait affirmer sa présence sur les chaînes de télévision, au cinéma ou sur Internet.** Alors que dans les années 70, les articles sur le design étaient l'apanage des magazines spécialisés, une première évolution a eu lieu dans les années 80, lorsque la presse grand public s'y intéressa de plus près. Et qu'en est-il des années 90? Le design ne devrait-il pas s'imposer à l'écran et toucher ainsi une plus large audience, dévoiler sa magie, sa multiplicité, son aspect créatif, son contenu narratif... Le jour où des émissions consacrées au design seront diffusées sur des chaînes de télévision telles que CNN, AOL ou MTV – on pourrait même imaginer que le design ait sa propre chaîne – alors, nous saurons ce jour-là que le design a triomphé. □ **Le design devrait être enseigné dans les meilleures écoles et universités de notre pays.** Alors que nous vivons de plus en plus dans un monde caractérisé par une surabondance d'images et de produits, aucune chaire de design n'a encore véritablement été créée. Le jour où le design industriel, les arts graphiques, l'illustration et la photographie auront trouvé la place qui leur revient dans les plus grandes universités américaines, alors, nous saurons ce jour-là que le design a triomphé.

STEVEN SKOV HOLT EST DIRECTEUR DE LA STRATÉGIE D'ENTREPRISE DE L'AGENCE FROGDESIGN À SUNNYVALE, CALIFORNIE, ET TITULAIRE D'UNE CHAIRE DE DESIGN INDUSTRIEL AU CALIFORNIA COLLEGE OF ARTS AND CRAFTS DE SAN FRANCISCO (CCAC).

Les étudiants en design pourraient étudier de plus près les besoins et le comportement humains. Au California College of Art and Crafts de San Francisco (CCAC), nous menons actuellement une étude sur la «post-adaptation» des produits par les consommateurs (Post-Market Product Alteration). L'objet de cette étude est de mieux appréhender le comportement des consommateurs en observant comment ces derniers adaptent les produits à leurs besoins. Le jour où graphistes et fabricants travailleront main dans la main pour mieux cerner les besoins et attentes du public – en analysant par exemple des phénomènes tels que la personnalisation des transistors, la mode des aimants décoratifs pour frigidaires, etc. – alors, nous saurons ce jour-là que le design a triomphé. □ **Le programme des études de design pourrait connaître une profonde réforme afin de supprimer l'inadéquation entre le savoir des étudiants diplômés et les exigences et besoins de leurs futurs employeurs.** On pourrait par exemple envisager de stimuler le travail d'équipe. Lorsque je songe en effet à l'envergure de certains projets de frogdesign et aux délais impartis, force est de reconnaître qu'une personne seule ne peut mener à bien de telles tâches. Si une forme de collaboration s'ensuit, si les travaux de recherche, la créativité, les prises de décision et l'apprentissage en équipe sont encouragés pour être au cœur même des programmes d'études, alors, nous saurons ce jour-là que le design a triomphé. □ **Le design pourrait également être enseigné dès le primaire ainsi que dans les hautes écoles d'économie.** Les enfants pourraient ainsi comprendre le rôle joué par le design dans notre société de consommation tandis que les futurs décideurs disposeraient d'un outil stratégique face à la concurrence. Lorsque des questions inhérentes aux produits comme la forme, la fonction ou la signification pourront être comprises et expliquées de tous, lorsque notre profession ne sera plus un domaine abstrait pour le grand public, alors, nous saurons ce jour-là que le design a triomphé. □ **Les professeurs de design pourraient s'atteler à une réforme des programmes d'études.** Peggy McIntosh, directrice d'un centre de recherches sur les femmes au Wellesley College, s'est engagée en faveur de méthodes d'apprentissage prônant la suppression de notions telles que réussite ou échec. Nous devons encourager le travail d'équipe et non plus un esprit de compétition égocentrique. Le jour où la formation des designers aura lieu dans un contexte convivial et ne s'apparentera plus à un concours où il n'y a qu'un seul gagnant, alors, nous saurons ce jour-là que le design a triomphé. □ **Les pro-fesseurs pourraient exploiter des idées, des projets à la lumière des enseignements de l'histoire du design et permettre ainsi aux étudiants de se forger leur propre conception du design.** Au CCAC, nous avons demandé à Barry Katz – spécialiste en histoire du design – d'expliquer aux étudiants les liens fondamentaux qui unissent l'histoire, la science des matériaux et le processus créatif. Le jour où nous réussirons à ne plus considérer l'histoire du design comme une sorte de hit-parade sans influence sur le processus créatif, alors, nous saurons ce jour-là que le design a triomphé. □ **Les postes fixes des professeurs pourraient être supprimés.** Nous pourrions investir – au niveau régional ou national – dans des pédagogues hautement compétents en leur demandant d'enseigner dans les grandes universités, la plupart (même parmi les plus élitaires des Etats-Unis) ne proposant pour l'heure aucun cursus en la matière. Pourrait-on en effet imaginer meilleur catalyseur pour une science encore jeune que de vrais pros de la branche et ce, précisément là où ils ont le plus d'impact? □ Le reste des enseignants, soit 95 %, pourraient être engagés à l'essai sur la base de leurs compétences. Cela correspond d'ailleurs aujourd'hui déjà à une réalité. De plus en plus, les personnes titulaires d'un savoir (designers ou professeurs par ex.) travaillent simultanément pour divers employeurs ou sur plusieurs projets. Le jour où l'enseignement pourra puiser à volonté dans le haut du panier des forces vives de la profession, alors, nous saurons ce jour-là que le design a triomphé – et, par là-même, la formation. □ Les designers – et plus particulièrement les étudiants en design – pourraient relever le grand défi de notre époque – l'hyperinformation – et tenter d'y apporter des solutions créatives. □ Au vu de notre société caractérisée par une surabondance d'informations, d'images et de produits, il est clair que le matériel informatique et le software vont devoir se faire plus «soft» pour mieux répondre, s'adapter aux besoins individuels de chacun. C'est ce qui transparaît aujourd'hui avec bonheur dans les pages de ce nouveau livre Graphis où la technologie – souple, flexible, malléable et durable – est parfaitement maîtrisée, prenant même parfois un peu de patine au fil des applications. Le résultat témoigne ainsi non seulement de l'essor d'une nouvelle industrie, d'un nouveau style, mais aussi de l'émergence d'une nouvelle génération de designers, la plus éveillée de tous les temps. Lorsque cette génération aura pris les rênes alors, nous saurons ce jour-là que le design a triomphé. Et nous saurons avec la même certitude qu'il nous faudra aussi, de la même manière, réinventer la culture visuelle. ■

What Should a Design School do for its Students? BY REBECA MÉNDEZ

PORTRAIT BY CATHLYN TAYLOR

"IN THE BEGINNER'S MIND THERE ARE MANY POSSIBILITIES, BUT IN THE EXPERT'S THERE ARE FEW."—ZEN MASTER SHUNRYU SUZUKI. □ To allow oneself not to know, to be ready for anything and open to everything is to have the mind of a beginner. In this not knowing, we may feel we've lost our balance as we lose our sense of knowing—we die, but at the same time we develop ourselves, we grow. It is here, in this instance of imbalance, that we can see things as if for the first time. □ Currently I am a graduate student in fine art, but I have been a designer since 1984, and a design director and educator at Art Center College of Design since 1985. This experience allows me to speak in a multiplicity of voices. This is appropriate for the subject of design education, which now more than ever requires multiple skills and a vast knowledge of culture. □ I entered the field of design after having been talked out of being a mathematician, a physicist, a dancer, and an architect. At fifteen I had no idea that by choosing a career I was also choosing a way of life. In many ways this life choice was already within me, as a sensitivity of perception and response to life, long before it was consolidated under "graphic design." I realize now, after 12 years of practicing design and five years as a fine artist, that there was a common thread through all those fields of study that attracted me so much when I was 15. It was being able to move the mind from this world into a world of extreme abstraction, and to transform that abstraction into something real through rigorous methodology. □ Passion and commitment are the two most important factors in any successful career choice, and these traits enable a student to go through the rigorous discipline of a design education. Thousands of hours are invested in learning the skills required to practice as a designer. But thinking as a designer requires an even greater investment of time and dedication—it is a life-long process. In 1984 I received a B.F.A. in graphic design after approximately two-and-a-half years, which seemed barely sufficient to acquire the necessary skills and definitely not enough time to form myself as a designer. The seeds are planted during college education, a backbone is formed, but the growth and the learning as a thinker/designer begin some time after graduation, when the mind is free from the task of learning the practical skills. Within this state of formlessness the spark of creativity ignites. The beginner's mind—the student's mind—is in the present; it is active. Knowledge is in the past, stored in memory, in a more passive state. *Pupil* has its origins in the Latin word *pupilla*—the circular opening in the iris of the eye through which light reaches the retina: the pupil as perpetual receptacle of light, whose perception and memory represent life. As a teacher, I have felt the student's mind as it moves from the preconceived to the unknown, and it is in that movement that the capacity for invention resides. □ I began a successful design practice with immediate recognition from the design community, but this didn't keep me from being deeply disappointed with my career choice which I saw as shallow and meaningless. In the working environment it is difficult to maintain a beginner's mind. In search of a more creative environment, I joined Art Center in 1989 as design director. At the same time, I began my graduate studies in fine art. I was able to approach design from another point of view. The exposure to critical thinking during my graduate studies, in conjunction with my work at Art Center, gave me the opportunity to re-examine the field of design and my role as a designer. □ An educational institution is in constant flux, always adapting to new technologies and thought. Being responsible for Art Center's visual identity has been an incredible challenge, for it is always in the process of change. Maintaining the fluidity of the beginner's mind has helped me continue to flow with this current. □ Being a good designer begins with knowing how to think. A life in design is a continual search for understanding, for meaning— observing and interpreting the signs from nature and culture, reorganizing and representing them in the desire to contribute to that culture. A life in design is about balancing intellectual inquiry with the physical production of design. Many students are choosing to continue their education in graduate studies, where they can further their own ideas and explore and articulate them through theory and practice. Whether it is through a mentor, an undergraduate or graduate education, or self-inquiry, exposure to critical thinking gives the design student the knowledge to move from mere decoration to design. □ New media and technologies continue to have dramatic cultural consequences, specifically with regard to the role of the designer, which changes and expands as these technologies become

REBECA MÉNDEZ WAS EDUCATED AT ART CENTER COLLEGE OF DESIGN IN PASADENA, CALIFORNIA. SHE GRADUATED IN 1984, REJOINED THE COLLEGE AS ITS DESIGNER IN 1989, AND BECAME DESIGN DIRECTOR IN 1991. SHE HAS TAUGHT GRAPHIC AND PACKAGING DESIGN SINCE 1985. MENDEZ HAS WON NUMEROUS DESIGN AWARDS, AND HER WORK IS INCLUDED THE PERMANENT COLLECTION OF THE LIBRARY OF CONGRESS AND OF THE COOPER-HEWITT NATIONAL DESIGN MUSEUM, SMITHSONIAN INSTITUTION, NEW YORK

readily accessible. It is critical for design schools to teach and work toward ecological sustainability. Designers are crucial in reassessing the way we inhabit this planet. We have to rethink our ways of communicating, the design practice, our role as designers, and our ways of teaching design. Not only is it the industry and the college's faculty which create new technolo-gies, but it is students who develop these technologies and construct the institution's culture. A design college should be able to provide a platform stable enough to sustain a creative environment while encouraging the movement of the beginner's mind—just as a riverbed holds the waters that run through it but also allows the power of its waters to change course. ■

Was sollte eine Design-Schule für ihre Studenten tun? VON REBECA MÉNDEZ

«Im Kopf des Anfängers gibt es viele Möglichkeiten, im Kopf des Experten nur wenige.» – Zen-Meister Shunryu Suzuki □ Sich selbst Unwissenheit zu erlauben, immer für alles bereit, für alles offen zu sein, heisst, den Geist eines Anfängers zu haben. In dieser Unwissenheit, wenn wir das Gefühl des Wissens verloren haben, geraten wir vielleicht aus dem Gleichgewicht – etwas stirbt, aber gleichzeitig wachsen wir. Was immer wir sehen verändert sich, verliert sein Gleichgewicht. Ich glaube, in diesem Moment der Unstabilität, können wir Dinge betrachten, als sähen wir sie zum ersten Mal. □ Da ich seit 1984 als Designerin arbeite, seit 1985 als Design Director und Pädagogin am Art Center College of Design und jetzt ausserdem Kunst studiere, kann ich die Dinge aus verschiedenen Perspektiven betrachten. Das ist beim Thema Design-Ausbildung ganz nützlich, denn mehr als je zuvor werden hier viele Fähigkeiten und ein breites Wissen im kulturellen Bereich verlangt. □ Ich entschied mich für Design, nachdem man mir ausgeredet hatte, Mathematik oder Physik oder Architektur zu studieren. Mit 15 Jahren war mir nicht bewusst, dass man in dem Moment, in dem man einen Beruf wählt, auch einen Lebenweg wählt. Ich wusste auch nicht, dass diese Wahl fürs Leben schon in mir war, in Form einer bestimmten Beobachtungsgabe und Reaktion auf das Leben, lange bevor es als Graphik-Design etikettiert wurde. Ich weiss heute, nachdem ich 15 Jahre als Designerin und 5 Jahre als Künstlerin gearbeitet habe, dass es unter all den Berufen, die mir als Fünfzehn-jährige vorschwebten, eine Verbindung gibt – und zwar die Fähigkeit zur extremen Abstraktion und Virtualität, die Fähigkeit, diese Abstraktion durch methodisches Vorgehen in etwas Tat-sächliches, Repräsentatives zu verwandeln, so dass die Antwort nicht nur auf einer rationalen Ebene, sondern auch auf einer sinnlichen erfassbar ist. □ Passion und Engagement sind zwei wichtige Faktoren bei einer erfolgreichen Berufswahl, und sie sind Voraussetzung dafür, dass der Student der rigorosen Diszi-plin einer Designausbildung gewachsen ist. Tausende von Stun-den werden auf das Erlernen des zur Ausübung des Berufes not-wendigen Handwerks verwendet. Aber noch mehr Zeit und Hin-gabe erfordert es, auch im Geiste ein Designer zu werden, es ist ein lebenslanger Prozess. 1984 erhielt ich den Titel BFA (Bachelor of Fine Arts) nach einem zweieinhalbjährigen Studium in Graphik-Design, gerade eben lang genug, um die notwendi-gen handwerklichen Fähigkeiten zu erlernen, und sicher nicht lang genug, um mich selbst zu einer Designerin zu entwickeln. Während der College-Ausbildung wird nur die Saat gelegt, das Rüstzeug mitgegeben, aber das Wachsen und das Lernen als reflektierender Designer beginnt erst einige Zeit nach dem Schulabschluss, wenn der Verstand vom Erlernen des Hand-werks befreit ist. □ Aber in diesem Stadium des noch nicht Ge-formtseins, in dem es noch keine festen Grenzen gibt, entzündet sich der Funke der Kreativität, denn wie kann man etwas kontrol-lieren, das noch keine Formen angenommen hat. Der Verstand des Designers, des Studenten befindet sich in der Gegenwart, er ist aktiv. Das Wissen liegt in der Vergangenheit, ist im Ge-dächtnis gespeichert, in einem eher passiven Zustand. Das englische Wort *Pupil* hat seinen Ursprung vom lateinischen *pupilla* – die Pupille, durch die das Licht auf die Netzhaut des Auges fällt. Der Schüler also als ständiger Empfänger von Licht, dessen Wahrnehmung und Erinnerung das Leben re-präsen-tieren. Als Lehrerin habe ich gespürt, wie sich der Geist der Schüler vom Vorgefassten zum Unbekannten hin bewegt, und ge-nau hier setzt die Phantasie, die Erfindungsgabe ein. □ Ich habe

REBECA MÉNDEZ SCHLOSS IHR STUDIUM 1984 AM ART CENTER COLLEGE OF DESIGN IN PASADENA, KALIFORNIEN, AB. 1989 WURDE SIE VON DIESEM COLLEGE ALS GRAPHIKERIN EINGESTELLT UND 1991 AVANCIERTE SIE ZUM DESIGN DIRECTOR. SEIT 1985 UNTERRICHTET SIE GRAPHIK UND VERPACKUNGSGESTALTUNG. FÜR IHRE ARBEITEN WURDE REBECA MÉNDEZ ALS BESTE IN DER GRAPHIK-KATEGORIE DES I.D. ANNUAL DESIGN REVIEW 1995 AUSGEZEICHNET SOWIE IN DER ONE HUNDRED SHOW DES AMERICAN CENTER OF DESIGN.

von Anfang an mit meinem Designbüro Erfolg gehabt, auch was die Anerkennung durch Kollegen angeht, aber das hinderte mich nicht, von meinem Beruf zutiefst enttäuscht zu sein, der mir hohl und bedeutungslos erschien. In der Arbeitswelt ist es schwer, sich den offenen Geist des Anfängers zu erhalten. Auf der Suche nach einem kreativen Umfeld ging ich 1989 als Design Director zum Art Center College of Design. Um mich weiterzubilden, begann ich gleichzeitig ein Kunststudium. Dadurch ist es mir möglich, Design unter einem anderen Blickwinkel zu sehen. Meine künstlerische Arbeit ist von meiner graphischen Arbeit durchdrungen. Die Anregung zu kritischem Denken, verbunden mit den aufregenden Entwicklungen im Design und in der Kommunikation in den vergangenen fünf Jahren, und meine Arbeit als Designerin für eine Design- und Kunstschule gaben mir die Möglichkeit, Design und meine Rolle als Designerin neu zu überdenken. □ Eine Schule ist in ständigem Fluss, sie hat sich ständig neuen Technologien und Denkweisen anzupassen. Es war daher eine grosse Herausforderung, für die visuelle Identität des Art Centers verantwortlich zu sein, weil es sich ständig weiterentwickelt. Es ist wie ein lebendiger Organismus, der pulsiert und atmet. Mir den Geist eines Anfängers zu bewahren hat mir geholfen, in diesem Strom mitzuschwimmen. □ Ein guter Designer zu sein beginnt damit, dass man gelernt hat, zu denken. Ein Leben im Design ist eine fortgesetzte Suche nach Verstehen, nach Bedeutung, nach Beobachtung und Interpretation von Zeichen der Natur und der Kultur, nach ihrer Neuanordnung und Darstellung, getragen von dem Wunsch, zur Kultur beizutragen. Ein Leben im Design heisst, die

intellektuelle Fragestellung mit der physischen Herstellung von Design zu verbinden. Viele Studenten entscheiden sich nach abgeschlossenem Studium für eine Fortsetzung ihrer Ausbildung, damit sie ihre eigenen Ideen verfolgen und sie in Theorie und Praxis untersuchen und artikulieren können. Sei es durch einen Mentor, durch eine Grundausbildung oder höheres Studium und/oder Selbstbefragung, nur durch Übung im kritischen Denken erkennt der Design-Student, wie er von reiner Dekoration zum Design gelangt. □ Neue Medien und Technologien haben weiterhin einschneidende kulturelle Konsequenzen, besonders auch im Hinblick auf die Rolle des Designs, die sich ständig verändert und erweitert, da diese Technologien für jedermann immer leichter zugänglich werden. Design-Schulen haben die Verpflichtung, ihren Unterricht und ihre Arbeit nach ökologischen Gesichtspunkten auszurichten. Designer sind aufgefordert, unseren Umgang mit unserem Planeten mit neuen Augen zu betrachten. Wir müssen unsere Kommunikationsformen überdenken, unsere Design-Praktiken, unsere Rolle als Designer und unseren Design-Unterricht. Nicht nur die Industrie und die Professoren eines Colleges schaffen neue Technologien, sondern es sind die Studenten, die diese Technologien entwickeln und zur Kultur eines Lehrinstituts beitragen. Ein Design-College sollte eine Plattform bieten, die stabil genug ist, um unter veränderten wirtschaftlichen und technologischen Voraussetzungen ein kreatives Umfeld zu erhalten und die Beweglichkeit des Geistes der Studienanfänger zu fördern, so wie ein Flussbett das Wasser aufnimmt, aber dem Strom erlaubt, seinen Lauf zu ändern. ∎

Quelle fonction doit remplir une école de design pour ses étudiants? PAR REBECA MÉNDEZ

«Dans l'esprit des débutants, il existe beaucoup de possibilités. Dans celui des experts, il y en a peu.» Le Maître Zen Shunryu Suzuki □ Rester dans l'incertitude, être toujours ouvert à tout ce qui se présente, cela s'appelle avoir l'esprit du débutant. Lorsque nous avons l'impression de ne pas savoir, nous sommes en situation de déséquilibre. Quelque chose meurt, mais en même temps quelque chose se développe en nous. Tout ce que nous voyons autour de nous se modifie en permanence. Or, je pense que c'est dans ces moments que

nous regardons les choses comme si nous les voyions pour la première fois. □ Etant donné que je travaille comme designer depuis 1984, que je suis directrice artistique de la promotion et enseignante au Art Center College of Design depuis 1989 et qu'en outre j'étudie actuellement l'histoire de l'art, je vois les choses sous différentes perspectives. Cela est très utile dans le domaine de la formation, car l'on exige de vous des connaissances de plus en plus étendues dans le domaine culturel. □ J'ai décidé de faire du design, après que l'on m'a

REBECA MÉNDEZ A OBTENU, EN 1984, SON DIPLÔME DU ART CENTER COLLEGE FOR DESIGN DE PASADENA, EN CALIFORNIE. EN 1989, ELLE A ÉTÉ ENGAGÉE COMME GRAPHISTE PAR CE MÊME ÉTABLISSEMENT, DONT ELLE EST DEVENUE, EN 1981, DESIGN DIRECTOR. ELLE Y ENSEIGNE DEPUIS 1985 LE GRAPHISME AINSI QUE LE GRAPHISME D'EMBALLAGE. ELLE A OBTENU LE 1ER PRIX DE L'I.D. ANNUAL DESIGN REVIEW DE 1995 DANS LA CATÉGORIE GRAPHISME AINSI QUE LE PRIX DU ONE HUNDRED SHOW DE L'AMERICAN CENTER OF DESIGN.

découragée d'étudier les mathématiques, la physique ou l'architecture. A quinze ans, je ne me rendais pas forcément compte que choisir une profession signifiait également choisir un style de vie. Je ne savais pas non plus que cette manière de vivre était en quelque sorte déjà en moi, sous forme d'une certaine sensibilité, d'un sens inné de l'observation et d'une manière de réagir aux choses, bien avant que j'y applique l'étiquette de design. Je réalise aujourd'hui, après 15 ans d'activité comme designer et cinq autres comme artiste, qu'il existe un lien entre toutes les professions qui m'attiraient à l'âge de quinze ans. C'est la possibilité de transposer la réalité tangible en une réalité abstraite, et ensuite, d'appliquer une méthodologie rigoureuse à cette abstraction pour en faire quelque chose de représentatif, qui parle aux sens aussi bien qu'à l'intellect. □ La passion et l'engagement sont deux aspects importants dans le choix réussi d'une carrière. Ce sont ces qualités qui motiveront l'étudiant à se soumettre à la discipline rigoureuse que requiert la formation de designer. Des milliers d'heures sont nécessaires pour acquérir la pratique inhérente au métier de graphiste. Mais il faut encore plus de temps et d'efforts pour devenir un designer dans sa tête. C'est un processus qui dure toute une vie. En 1984, j'ai obtenu mon BFA (Bachelor of Fine Arts), après deux ans et demi d'études dans le domaine du graphisme, tout juste assez de temps pour acquérir les bases pratiques, mais certainement pas assez pour devenir designer. Durant sa formation, on ne fait que planter les graines, ou créer l'ossature de sa future profession. Ce n'est que plus tard, après le diplôme, que l'on commence à développer sa propre réflexion sur le design, lorsque l'esprit est libéré de l'obligation d'apprendre. □ Après cette phase un peu transitoire, où les frontières sont encore floues, s'allume tout à coup le feu de la créativité. Car comment contrôler quelque chose qui est encore informe? L'esprit du débutant ou de l'étudiant est axé sur le présent, il est actif. La connaissance appartient au passé, elle est stockée dans la mémoire à l'état passif. Le terme anglais *pupil* pour désigner l'étudiant, trouve son origine dans le mot latin *pupilla* – l'ouverture dans l'iris de l'œil qui permet à la lumière d'atteindre la rétine. L'étudiant est donc un réceptacle pour la lumière. En tant qu'enseignante, j'ai pu observer comment l'esprit des étudiants progresse du connu vers l'inconnu. C'est dans ce mouvement que réside la capacité à inventer. □ Lorsque j'ai ouvert mon atelier de design, j'ai obtenu immédiatement le succès ainsi que la reconnaissance de mes pairs.

Mais cela ne m'a pas empêchée de me sentir parfois déçue par mon choix professionnel. Une fois dans le monde du travail, il est difficile de préserver l'esprit du débutant. Aussi, c'est dans le but de pouvoir travailler dans un environnement très créatif que j'ai rejoint l'équipe du Art Center College of Design comme enseignante et directrice artistique en 1989. Afin de compléter mon éducation, j'ai parallèlement entrepris des études en histoire de l'art. De cette manière, il m'est possible de porter un autre regard sur le design, même si mon travail artistique est évidemment influencé par mon travail graphique. La pensée critique développée au cours de mes études, les transformations fascinantes que subissent actuellement la profession de graphiste et tout le domaine de la communication, ainsi que mon travail d'enseignante au sein d'une école d'art et de design m'ont offert la possibilité de réfléchir différemment au rôle et à la fonction du designer. □ Etre un bon designer c'est d'abord savoir réfléchir. C'est une profession dans laquelle l'on est constamment en train d'observer et d'interpréter les signes de la nature et de la culture, afin de réorganiser ces signes et de contribuer à la culture par leur représentation. Le design, c'est relier la réflexion à une production tangible. Beaucoup d'étudiants décident, après leurs études de base, de poursuivre leur formation pour développer leurs propres idées et les confronter à des expériences concrètes. □ Les nouveaux médias et technologies ont des conséquences culturelles considérables, en particulier sur le rôle des designers qui se modifie et s'étend au fur et à mesure que ces technologies deviennent plus accessibles à tout un chacun. Les écoles de design ont également la responsabilité d'enseigner des techniques qui soient respectueuses de notre environnement. Les designers jouent un rôle central dans la manière dont nous concevons nos rapports avec notre cadre de vie. Nous devons repenser notre manière de communiquer, nos techniques de travail, le rôle de notre profession et de la formation. Ce n'est pas seulement l'industrie et les professeurs qui créent les nouvelles technologies, mais aussi les étudiants qui contribuent à les développer et à en faire un élément intrinsèque de la culture de notre institution. Une école de design devrait pouvoir offrir une plateforme suffisamment stable pour assurer un environnement créatif à travers toutes les mutations technologiques et économiques que nous connaissons actuellement. Et surtout, les écoles doivent encourager la fraîcheur d'esprit qui caractérise le débutant. L'école doit être comme le lit d'une rivière, qui guide l'écoulement de l'eau tout en lui permettant de changer de cours. ∎

Don't panic—the world won't stop moving! BY UWE LOESCH

What we have here is a book full of work by students who, page after page, show us what is going on in the way of communication design at institutes and universities all over the world. Yet it is a self-contained world, one that seems to revolve on its own axis. □ As such, these works present an ant's view of more or less completely computer-assisted, commercial art. Nevertheless, it seems to me that B. Martin Pedersen wants this book to be a broad overview—an in-depth examination of the shuttle between the old and new worlds. □ For several years now, we have been able to confound measurable time on the Internet by aiming virtual snowballs at students from Upsala University, or retorting electronically against the prevailing spirit of the times. Graphic designers already define their profession as the interface between message and medium. However, it is not that easy to translate language into an image. □ In a sense, both the printed word and image are pure illusion. In this book, however, they come across with the power of reality. Graphic design, a product of our culture, is limited by serving a common denominator. It requires taxing anticipation of, and compliance with, the demands of the "master"—be it a client, a firm, or the media—as opposed to fine art, which must answer only to itself. □ Graphic designers are more or less serious people who unfortunately tend to take themselves too seriously. In creating an image of this world for themselves and others, they are, however, expected to achieve something more than an impression of the inherently abstract world of our mind's eye. They are obliged to surf the fashion waves of the day in art and design. Or else the little rascals skate the (ever so thin) ice of puddles, skimming a surface fraught with personal "significance" and vital only to sustaining their own ideas. This becomes all the more problematic when design is commercialized and becomes a substitute identity for globally interchangeable messages, services, and wares—becoming a consumer ware itself. Graphic design can thus contribute as much to environmental pollution as architecture or garbage. This takes more than a lack of ideas—sometimes it takes being incapable of expressing them. The intent here is as cynical as it is serious. For if we do not learn to keep a critical distance with respect to our design works, what we do is worth less than the honorable output of the humblest of crafts. □ The widespread influence attributed to marketing and publicity gives some communication designers an exaggerated opinion of themselves, even a feeling of omnipotence. Misrepresentation has long been considered by some to be an acceptable method of startling the public out of its habitual lethargy. Given the scabrous nature of what does hit the press, we would be well advised not to leave the interpretation of our world either to some firm's "United Colors" or to the "ayatollahs" of the design world. □ The best of the institutes and universities of communication design are hence those that provide, above all, a framework for the coming to terms with our physical world and for dialogue with our other—online—world. Since creativity can not be learned, and hence not taught, student training involves producing copies. This copycat technique does, however, need to be learned. Even "Troy" (William Henry Gates III) first took a degree in "law and order" before turning the world topsy-turvy. Rumor has it he was a real nerd, an "eager-beaver," and is now taking his revenge on the dumb public by providing them with a "window" through which to gawk at an even narrower version of the world. That "face-lifter," Neville Brody, was sent flying on his ear by his School of Typography. Meanwhile, David Carson, after sailing through the design department of San Diego State University and Oregon College of Commercial Art, disappeared in three weeks time—hippety hop—into the realm of Hans Rudolf Lutz in Rapperswill. It would be worthwhile knowing what sort of a utilitarian dogmatist could have gotten Brody fired, and who could offer the sort of opposition to Carson that would incite him to come up with his own uniquely personal language. For above all, creativity is meant to be understood—and celebrated—as something of a conquest over the traditional view of the world! □ Ludwig Wittgenstein once asked a student at Cambridge how man came to visualize the sun as revolving around the earth. "Because that's the way it looks," the student answered. To which Wittgenstein retorted: "What would it look like if the earth revolved around the sun?" ■

UWE LOESCH IS BASED IN DÜSSELDORF, GERMANY. HE TEACHES COMMUNICATION DESIGN AT THE BERGISCHE UNIVERSITÄT WUPPERTAL. AS A VISITING PROFESSOR, HE HAS LECTURED AND CONDUCTED WORKSHOPS IN CANADA, CHINA, JAPAN, HONG KONG, SINGAPORE, ISRAEL, INDONESIA, IRELAND, ENGLAND, SCOTLAND, FRANCE, SPAIN, ITALY, SWEDEN, FINLAND, POLAND, BULGARIA, RUSSIA AND THE UNITED STATES. HE IS A MEMBER OF THE AGI (ALLIANCE GRAPHIQUE INTERNATIONALE).

Don't panic - it moves! Oder: Keine Panik – sie dreht sich doch! VON UWE LOESCH

Das da in Ihren Händen ist ein Buch voller bunter Bilder, die sich entgegen dem Uhrzeigersinn, aber mit der Welt, von links nach rechts geblättert, um sich selbst drehen. □ Es sind Arbeiten von Studierenden, die seitenweise über den Stand der Dinge des Kommunikations-Designs an Hochschulen und Universitäten in und aus aller Welt berichten. □ So gesehen vermitteln sie eine Weltanschauung aus der Froschperspektive der mehr oder weniger computergestützten Gebrauchsgraphik. Nichts destoweniger stelle ich mir vor, dass der Herausgeber B. Martin Pedersen dieses erste Opus *Graphis Student Design 96* in 10 000 m Höhe aus der Vogelperspektive als Pendler zwischen der Alten und der Neuen Welt konzipiert hat. □ Hierfür müssen wir ihm und seinen Mitwisserinnen vorerst herzlich danken, denn das Zusammentragen, Sichten und Auswählen dieser vielen Ansprüche auf «Sehen und Gesehen werden» ist eine verantwortungsvolle Tätigkeit zwischen Lust und Qual. □ Zum Glück kann *Graphis Student Design 96* nur einen ersten Ausschnitt im Anschnitt bieten. Irgendwann liegen die Themen, lieber Martin, «in der Luft», und *Graphis Student Design 96* ist beinahe so aktuell wie überflüssig. Längst können wir auf absehbare Zeit con-fuse im Internet mit virtuellen Schneebällen auf die Studierenden der Universität von Upsala schiessen, oder mit Dattelkernen in Jalalabad oder Ouagadougou der Zeit den Geist hinterherwerfen. □ Schon rechtfertigt der Graphik-Designer seinen Berufsstand als Schnittstelle zwischen Botschaft und Medium. Dabei ist es gar nicht so einfach, erst einmal Sprache als Bild wahrzunehmen und Bild als Abbild zu begreifen. □ Das gedruckte Wort und Bild jedoch ist die Täuschung schlechthin. Es hat den Anschein, fix und fertig zu sein und dokumentiert auch in diesem Buch die Macht des Faktischen. Denn die Kulturtechnik Graphik-Design begrenzt sich in ihrer Selbstähnlichkeit. Im Gegensatz zur freien Kunst, die nur sich selbst verpflichtet ist, erschöpft sich der Graphiker in vorauseilendem Gehorsam gegenüber dem «Meister», dem Auftraggeber oder der Gesellschaft und nicht zuletzt gegenüber den Medien. □ Graphik-Designer sind mehr oder weniger gebildet – vor allem aber sind sie eingebildet. Sich und anderen ein Bild von dieser Welt vormachen zu wollen, bedeutet eben doch erheblich mehr, als ein virtuelles Abziehbild der Oberfläche, dieser «Kraft-unseres-Geistes-an-und-für-sich-wunder-bar-wahrnehmbaren-Welt», zu schaffen. □ Graphiker, so müssen wir statt dessen annehmen, sind Surfer auf der jeweiligen Modewelle der Kunst oder des Designs. Sie sind das Büblein auf dem (dünnen) Eis der Pfütze, die man für bedeutend und für die Tragfähigkeit der eigenen Gedanken und Ideen für unentbehrlich hält. □ Dies wird um so problematischer, wenn der Wirtschaftsfaktor Design zum Identitätsersatz von weltweit austauschbaren Botschaften, Dienstleistungen und Waren verantwortet werden muss und so selbst zur Ware wird. Graphik-Design kann zum Beispiel ebenso zur visuellen Umweltverschmutzung beitragen wie Architektur oder Müll. □ Es genügt deshalb nicht, keine Ideen zu haben, man muss auch manchmal unfähig sein, sie ausdrücken zu können. □ Das ist so zynisch wie ernst gemeint. Denn wenn wir nicht lernen, mit ironisch-kritischer Distanz unsere Machwerke zu betrachten, sind wir weniger als Friseure, die immerhin ein ehrbares Handwerk ausüben. □ Der Einfluss auf viele Menschen, der Marketing und Werbung zugeschrieben wird, führt bei so manchem Kommunikations-Designer zur Selbstüberschätzung oder gar zu Allmachtsvorstellungen. Tausch und Täuschung gelten längst als Legitimation für Erregung von Aufmerksamkeit bei der Überwindung der Langeweile. Angesichts dieser veröffentlichten Ärgernisse dürfen wir die Interpretation unserer Welt weder den «Vereinigten Farben» einer Firma überlassen, noch den «Ajatollahs» unter den Designern anvertrauen. □ Hochschulen für Kommunikations-Design, die besten allzumal, sind deshalb Gehäuse, die vor allem Raum für die kontroverse Auseinandersetzung mit dieser einen Welt bieten müssen und den Dialog in jener anderen verkabelten Welt fördern sollten. Da Kreativität nicht erlernbar und damit auch nicht lehrbar ist, übt sich der Studierende in der Herstellung von Kopien (dieser Welt). Dieses Nachlallen will jedoch gelernt sein. Obwohl uns die Neuen Medien vormachen wollen, Gestaltung sei ein unbedingter Reflex. □ Auch «Trey» (William Henry Gates III.) hat erst einmal auf einer Universität «Recht und Ordnung» studiert, bevor er die Welt durcheinanderbrachte. Er soll als Kid ein «Nerd», ein «Streber» gewesen sein, der nun aus Rache das dumme Volk aus dem «Fenster» in die Traufe gucken lässt. □ Der Face-Lifter Neville Brody flog aus seiner Kunstdruck-Schule, während David Carson über Jahre durch das Design Department der San Diego State University und das Oregon College of Commercial Art surfte, bis er hip hop in drei Wochen unter anderem bei Hans Rudolf Lutz in Rapperswil untertauchte. □ Es wäre wert zu wissen, welcher Nützlichkeitsfanatiker Neville gefeuert hat und wer David

UWE LOESCH DÜSSELDORF, GERMANY, LEHRT AN DER BERGISCHEN UNIVERSITÄT WUPPERTAL ALS PROFESSOR FÜR KOMMUNIKATIONS-DESIGN UND WAR ALS GASTPROFESSOR ZU VORTRÄGEN UND WORKSHOPS IN CANADA, CHINA, JAPAN, HONG KONG, SINGAPUR, ISRAEL, INDONESIEN, IRLAND, ENGLAND, SCHOTTLAND, FRANKREICH, SPANIEN, ITALIEN, SCHWEDEN, FINNLAND, POLEN, BULGARIEN, RUSSLAND UND DEN USA UNTERWEGS. ER IST MITGLIED DER AGI – ALLIANCE GRAPHIQUE INTERNATIONALE.

jenen notwendigen Widerstand bot, der eine eigene unverwechselbare Sprache provoziert. Denn Kreativität müssen wir vor allem als Ausdruck von Überwindung traditioneller Weltanschauung begreifen und feiern! □ Ludwig Wittgenstein fragte einst in Cambridge einen Studenten, wie der Mensch auf die Vorstellung gekommen sei, dass sich die Sonne um die Erde dreht. «Weil es so aussieht» antwortete der Student. Darauf Wittgenstein: «Wie würde es aussehen, wenn sich die Erde um die Sonne dreht?» ∎

Don't panic – it moves! Pas de panique – elle tourne quand même! PAR UWE LOESCH

Ce que vous tenez entre les mains est un livre, un livre rempli d'images en couleur qui, feuilletées de gauche à droite, c'est-à-dire dans le sens opposé aux aiguilles d'une montre, tournent sur elles-mêmes en épousant le mouvement de rotation de la Terre. Il s'agit de travaux d'étudiants du monde entier qui, page après page, brossent un vaste panorama de ce qui se fait actuellement en matière de graphisme de communication dans les hautes écoles et universités de la planète. □ On y voit, autrement dit, l'univers du graphisme publicitaire, plus ou moins assisté par ordinateur, tel qu'il apparaît aujourd'hui en ce bas monde. Je suis pourtant prêt à parier que son éditeur, B. Martin Pedersen, a conçu ce premier numéro de *Graphis Student Design* à 10 000 mètres d'altitude, lors des fréquentes navettes qu'il effectue entre l'Ancien et le Nouveau Monde. □ Mais avant de poursuivre, remercions-le tout d'abord, lui et ses collaboratrices; assembler, visionner et sélectionner un tel matériel est, en effet, un tour de force lourd de responsabilités, à la limite du plaisir et de la torture. □ Heureusement que *Graphis Student Design* ne peut en présenter qu'un premier extrait. En effet, mon cher Martin, ces sujets ont tous été véhiculés un jour ou l'autre par l'air du temps, rendant *Graphis Student Design* presque aussi actuel que superflu. Cela fait belle lurette que nous pouvons, par Internet interposé, bombarder de boules de neige virtuelles les étudiants de l'Université d'Upsala ou planter nos choux à Djelal-Abad ou Ouagadougou. □ Déjà, le graphiste justifie sa fonction en se présentant comme l'interface entre le message et le média. Dieu sait, pourtant, qu'il n'est pas si simple de recevoir la parole sous forme d'image et de se dire que l'image est représentation. □ Mais le mot et l'image imprimés, voilà assurément le degré suprême de l'imposture. Ils ont l'apparence du définitif et témoignent, dans ce livre comme dans tous les autres, du pouvoir qu'exerce le factuel. Car le graphisme est borné par sa ressemblance avec lui-même. Contrairement à l'artiste libre, qui n'a de compte à rendre qu'à lui-même, le graphiste s'épuise à devancer les désirs du «maître», du client ou de la société, sans oublier, bien évidemment, les médias. □ Souvent cultivé, le graphiste est surtout prétentieux. Si déjà il se fait fort de se donner à soi-même, ainsi qu'à ses semblables, une image du monde dans lequel nous vivons, on attend autre chose de lui qu'une décalcomanie virtuelle de la surface de ce «monde-que-notre-esprit-nous-rend-si-merveilleusement-perceptible». □ Au lieu de quoi le graphiste surfe, selon toute apparence, sur les tendances à la mode de l'art et du design ou danse et virevolte sur la glace des flaques, effleurant de la lame de ses patins la mince couche de ses certitudes. □ Là où les choses se corsent, c'est lorsque le graphisme publicitaire se mue en substitut d'identité pour des messages, des services et des marchandises interchangeables et, ce faisant, devient à son tour une marchandise. Le graphisme peut, au même titre que l'architecture ou un dépôt d'ordures, contribuer à la pollution visuelle de l'environnement. Il ne suffit donc pas d'être en panne d'idées, quelquefois il faut aussi avoir l'élégance d'être incapable de les exprimer. □ Je dis cela avec autant de sérieux que de cynisme. Si nous n'apprenons pas à considérer le fruit de nos élucubrations avec une distance critique et ironique, nous sommes moins que le plus humble des artisans. □ L'influence que le marketing et la publicité sont censés exercer sur tant de gens conduit bien des graphistes de communication à se prendre pour plus grands qu'ils ne sont, voire à se croire tout-puissants. Tous les coups ne sont-ils pas permis dès lors qu'il s'agit d'attirer l'attention et de vaincre l'ennui? Tirant la leçon de ces sujets d'irritation, gardons-nous d'abandonner l'interprétation de notre monde aux «couleurs réunies» d'une quelconque entreprise ou aux «aya-

UWE LOESCH, DÜSSELDORF, ALLEMAGNE, EST PROFESSEUR DE GRAPHISME DE COMMUNICATION À LA BERGISCHE UNIVERSITÄT WUPPERTAL. IL A DONNÉ DES CONFÉRENCES ET DIRIGÉ DES ATELIERS COMME PROFESSEUR INVITÉ AU CANADA, EN CHINE, AU JAPON, À HONG KONG, À SINGAPOUR, EN ISRAËL, EN INDONÉSIE, EN IRLANDE, EN ANGLETERRE, EN ECOSSE, EN FRANCE, EN ESPAGNE, EN ITALIE, EN SUÈDE, EN FINLANDE, EN POLOGNE, EN BULGARIE, EN RUSSIE ET AUX ETATS-UNIS. IL EST MEMBRE DE L'AGI.

tollahs» de la publicité. □ Aussi les meilleures écoles de graphisme de communication sont-elles des lieux où l'on privilégie le débat contradictoire sur les sujets qui agitent ce monde et cultive le dialogue avec cet autre monde qu'est celui du câble. Comme la créativité ne s'apprend pas plus qu'elle ne s'enseigne, l'étudiant se fait la main en produisant des copies (de ce monde). Or, n'en déplaise aux nouveaux médias qui veulent nous faire croire que créer est un acte spontané, même singer est une activité que l'on ne peut exercer sans l'avoir apprise. □ Même «Troy» (William Henry Gates III) a étudié le droit dans une université avant de mettre le monde sens dessus dessous. Enfant, il n'y avait, paraît-il, pas plus bûcheur que lui, et c'est uniquement par vengeance qu'il condamne le peuple ignare à ouvrir et fermer à longueur de journée des fenêtres qui rétrécissent encore notre vision de l'univers. □ Grand spécialiste du lifting, Neville Brody a été renvoyé d'une école d'impression d'art, David Carson a longtemps usé ses jeans sur les bancs du département d'arts graphiques de San Diego State University et de l'Oregon College of Commercial Art avant que Hans Rudolf Lutz ne le fasse venir à Rapperswil. □ Il serait intéressant de connaître le monstre d'utilitarisme qui a mis Neville à la porte et de savoir qui a opposé à David la résistance dont a résulté ce langage qui n'appartient qu'à lui. Qu'est-ce, en effet, que la créativité sinon la marque de celui qui a surmonté les idées reçues? C'est ainsi qu'il faut la voir et la célébrer. □ Un jour, Ludwig Wittgenstein demande à un élève de Cambridge comment l'homme avait pu imaginer que le Soleil tournait autour de la Terre. «Parce ce que ça en a tout l'air», répond l'étudiant. Alors Wittgenstein: «Et de quoi aurait-ce l'air si la Terre tournait autour du Soleil?» ■

■ UWE LOESCH WITH STUDENTS FROM THE SWIRE SCHOOL OF DESIGN, HONG KONG. ● UWE LOESCH MIT STUDENTEN DER SWIRE SCHOOL OF DESIGN, HONG KONG. ▲ UWE LOESCH AVEC DES ÉTUDIANTS DE LA SWIRE SCHOOL OF DESIGN, HONG KONG.

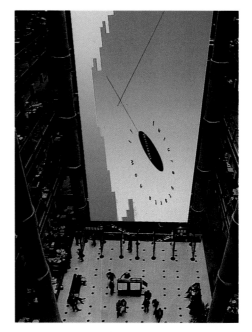

■ **1–6** Student: MATTHIAS BOIE College: FACHHOCHSCHULE RHEINLAND-PFALZ, ABT. MAINZ 1 Degree: CORPORATE IDENTITY DESIGN Professor: OLAF LEU Class: GRADUATE THESIS Country: GERMANY ■ **7** Student: CHRISTOPHER TURNER College: SCHOOL OF VISUAL ARTS Degree: ADVERTISING Professor: RICH OSTROFF Country: USA ■ (FOLLOWING SPREAD LEFT PAGE AND RIGHT PAGE,

THE COCKPIT GETS SO LOUD YOU WON'T EVEN HEAR YOUR PASSENGER SCREAM.

Ferrari does not usually promote speeding, disruption of family picnics, waking up the neighbors or torture to fellow passengers. Call 1 800 477 5626 for your nearest Ferrari dealer.

TOP) ■ **1, 2** Student: ISTVÁN LABADY College: THE ACADEMY OF CRAFTS AND DESIGN Degree: PHOTOGRAPHY Professor: BELA TOTH Class: 6TH TERM Country: HUNGARY ■ (FOLLOWING SPREAD RIGHT PAGE BOTTOM) **3** Student: MARIA LAHANIDOY College: VAKALO SCHOOL OF ART AND DESIGN Degree: GRAPHIC DESIGN Professor: D. PSOMAS, S. SIMEONIDES Class: 3RD TERM Country: GREECE

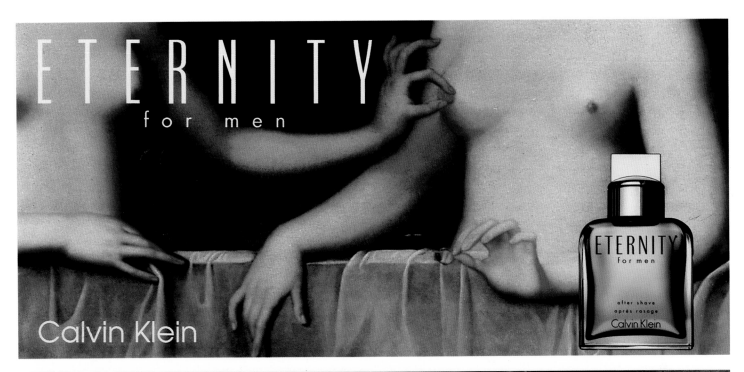

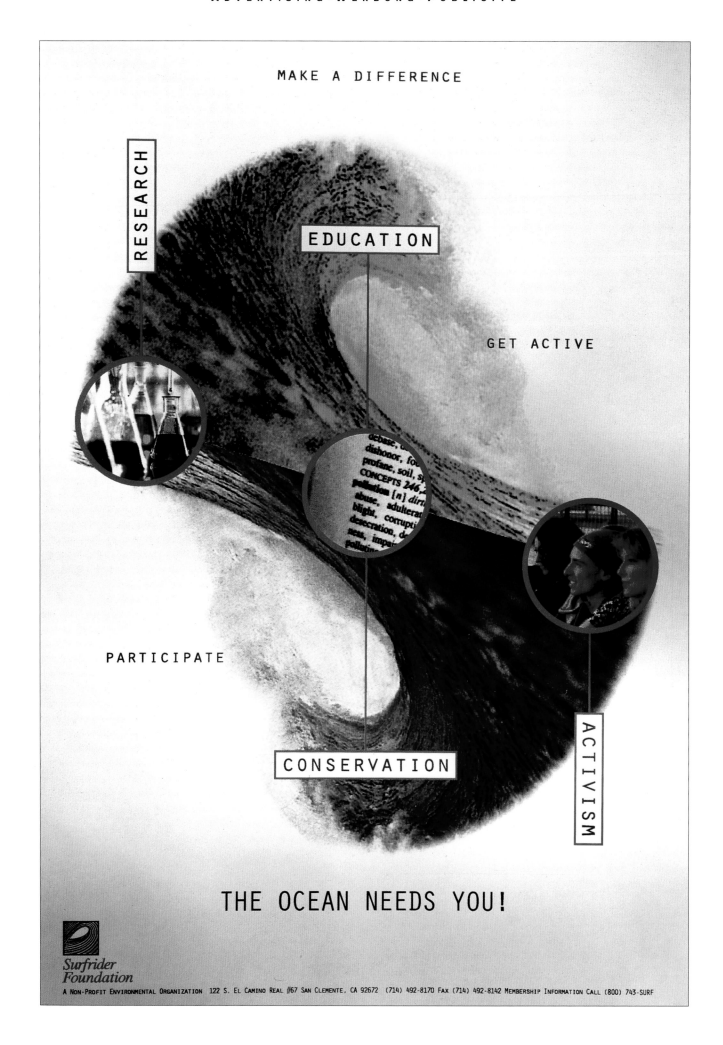

■ (ABOVE) **1, 2** STUDENT: CLAUDE LABRIE COLLEGE: UNIVERSITÉ DU QUÉBEC À MONTRÉAL DEGREE: BA IN GRAPHIC DESIGN PROFESSOR: FRÉDÉRIC METZ CLASS: GRAPHIC DESIGN: EXPERIMENT COUNTRY: CANADA ■ (OPPOSITE PAGE TOP) **3, 4** STUDENT: MILER HUNG COLLEGE: TEXAS CHRISTIAN UNIVERSITY PROFESSOR: ALAN LIDJI CLASS: AD II COUNTRY: USA ■ (OPPOSITE PAGE, BOTTOM LEFT) **5** STUDENT: GEORGE STAMOULIS COLLEGE: VAKALO SCHOOL OF ART AND DESIGN DEGREE: GRAPHIC DESIGN PROFESSOR: D. PSOMAS, S. SIMEONIDES CLASS: 3RD YEAR COUNTRY: GREECE ■(OPPOSITE PAGE, BOTTOM RIGHT) **6** STUDENT: ELENA KACHRILAS COLLEGE: VAKALO SCHOOL OF ART AND DESIGN DEGREE: GRAPHIC DESIGN PROFESSOR: D. PSOMAS, S. SIMEONIDES CLASS: 3RD YEAR COUNTRY: GREECE

HAGGAR

Wrinkle free pants.

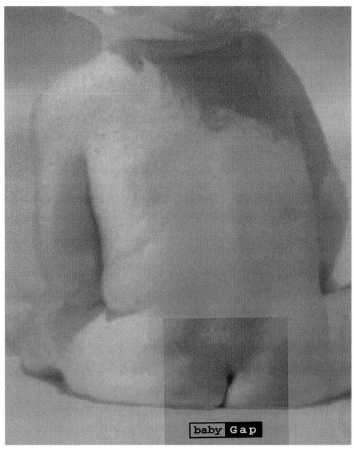

baby Gap

NIKE

Living dangerously?

DUREX

(THIS SPREAD)

STUDENT: DORON EDUT

COLLEGE: SCHOOL OF VISUAL ARTS

DEGREE: BFA

PROFESSOR: JEFFREY METZNER

COUNTRY: USA

Today the consistent

this tea is maintained

by the skill

of Lipton's buyers and

blenders who select only the

finest tea for Yellow Label.

ONE MORE WEEK

σαν τον παλιό καλό καιρό...

■ 1 STUDENT: ARGIRO MERSINIA COLLEGE: VAKALO SCHOOL OF ART AND DESIGN DEGREE: GRAPHIC DESIGN PROFESSOR: D. PSOMAS, S. SIMEONIDES CLASS: 3RD YEAR COUNTRY: GREECE ■ 2 STUDENT: GEORGE KRANITIS COLLEGE: VAKALO SCHOOL OF ART AND DESIGN DEGREE: GRAPHIC DESIGN PROFESSOR: D. PSOMAS, S. SIMEONIDES CLASS: 3RD YEAR COUNTRY: GREECE ■ 3 STUDENT: MICHAEL TOWELL COLLEGE: PORTFOLIO CENTER, GEORGIA DEGREE: ADVERTISING COUNTRY: USA ■ 4 STUDENT: MARIA DELIGIORGI COLLEGE: VAKALO

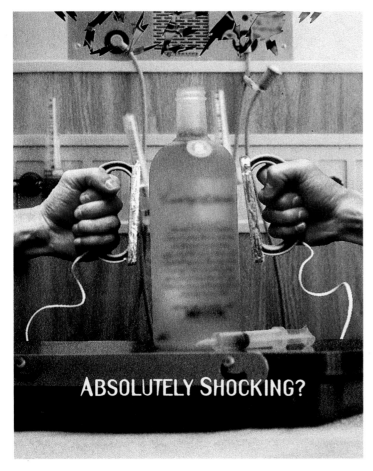

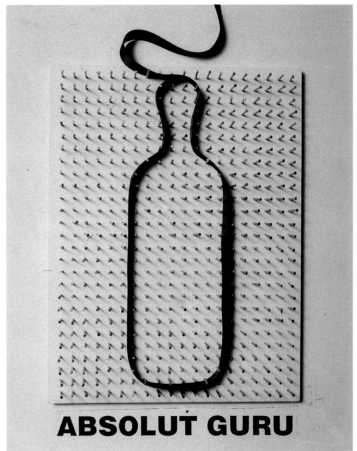

SCHOOL OF ART AND DESIGN DEGREE: GRAPHIC DESIGN PROFESSOR: D. PSOMAS, S. SIMEONIDES CLASS: 3RD YEAR COUNTRY: GREECE ■ 5 STUDENTS: RYAN GREEN, BRIAN WARD, SHANNON YOCUM, GAYANNA PONSER PHOTOGRAPHER: BRIAN WARD ILLUSTRATORS: RYAN GREEN, BRIAN WARD COPYWRITERS: RYAN GREEN, GAYANNA PONSER COLLEGE: BOWLING GREEN STATE UNIVERSITY DEGREE: GRAPHIC DESIGN PROFESSOR: SHERWOOD MCBROOM CLASS: ADVERTISING DESIGN COUNTRY: USA ■ 6 STUDENT: GELINA AVGERINOU COLLEGE: VAKALO SCHOOL OF ART AND DESIGN DEGREE: GRAPHIC DESIGN PROFESSOR: D. PSOMAS, S. SIMEONIDES CLASS: 3RD YEAR COUNTRY: GREECE

All of the people
some of the time.

TOWER RECORDS

■ (PRECEDING SPREAD ALL IMAGES) **1–4** Student: SUSANNE GRAF College: AKADEMIE DER BILDENDEN KÜNSTE STUTTGART Degree: GRAPHIC DESIGN Professor: HEINZ EDELMANN Class: 12TH TERM Country: GERMANY ■ (THIS PAGE) **1** Student: MICHAEL R. VELLA College: SCHOOL OF VISUAL ARTS Degree: BFA Professors: DAVID STERLING, JEFFREY METZNER Country: USA ■ (OPPOSITE PAGE TOP LEFT) **2** Student: ANESTIS BITSIKAS College: VAKALO SCHOOL OF ART AND DESIGN Degree: GRAPHIC DESIGN Professor: D. PSOMAS, S. SIMEONIDES Class: 3RD YEAR Country: GREECE ■ (OPPOSITE PAGE TOP RIGHT AND BOTTOM LEFT AND RIGHT) **3–5** Student: OMAR LEE College: PRATT INSTITUTE Degree: BFA Country: USA

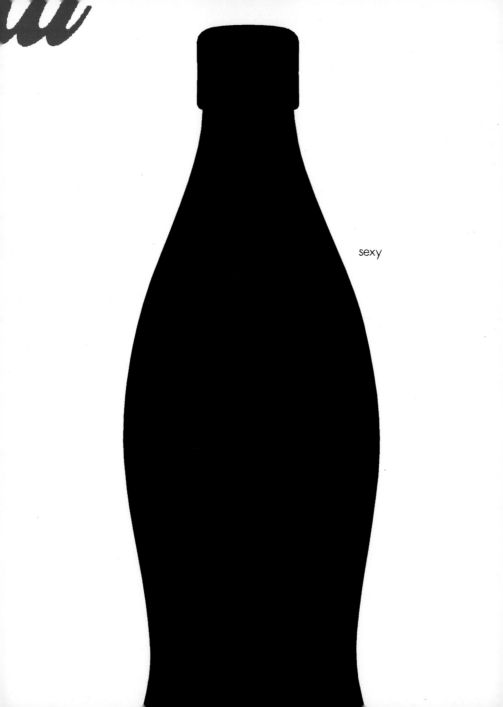

sexy

sexy

sexy

■ (PRECEDING SPREAD) **1–3** STUDENT: DORON EDUT COLLEGE: SCHOOL OF VISUAL ARTS DEGREE: BFA PROFESSOR: JEFFREY METZNER COUNTRY: USA ■ (THIS PAGE) **1–4** STUDENT: HANS HEINRICH SURES COLLEGE: FACHHOCHSCHULE DORTMUND DEGREE: FACHBEREICH DESIGN PROFESSOR: H.D. SCHRADER CLASS: 10TH TERM COUNTRY: GERMANY ■ (OPPOSITE PAGE TOP LEFT AND

RIGHT AND BOTTOM LEFT) **5–7** STUDENT: BRIAN J. SINGER COLLEGE: CALIFORNIA POLYTECHNIC STATE UNIVERSITY DEGREE: BA PROFESSOR: MARY LAPORTE CLASS: ADVERTISING DESIGN COUNTRY: USA ■ (OPPOSITE PAGE BOTTOM RIGHT) **8** STUDENT: MICHAEL R. VELLA COLLEGE: SCHOOL OF VISUAL ARTS DEGREE: BFA PROFESSORS: DAVID STERLING, JEFFREY METZNER COUNTRY: USA

Los Angeles

 San Francisco

 San Jose

 Fresno

 Bakersfield

 *San Luis Obispo*

Come Sit In Our Chairs

 Los Angeles

 San Francisco

 San Jose

 Fresno

 Bakersfield

 San Luis Obispo

Come Fill Up Our Briefcases

 Los Angeles

 San Francisco

San Jose

Fresno

 Bakersfield

 San Luis Obispo

Come Walk In Our Shoes

STATEN ISLAND BOTANICAL GARDEN

The meek shall inherit the earth,
and that should be
good enough for them.

Peaks this high are reserved for the strong. The highly motivated. And for no one else. With that in mind, we've designed the Dana Design Terraplane. Definitely

succeed where other packs most often fail: fit. It's made with high density carbon stays and a polyethylene framesheet. The resulting flex distributes weight to your hips and away from your back.

This means a perfect fit.

Fabric tough enough to endure all types of hellish conditions. If you happen to be going that way.

We could go on for days, but you probably don't have time to read that long.

ArcFlex design couples high density carbon fiber stays and a polyethylene framesheet. The resulting flex moves weight from your back to your hips.

the right pack to carry where other packs just can't cut it. It was created by serious climbers, who know what you'll go through to get to the top.

The Terraplane utilizes ArcFlex technology to

and guarantees the Terraplane will feel like part of your body.

Just as much as a pack can.

And durability isn't just something we've thrown by the wayside. The outer shell is 1000 Denier Cordura Plus. The strongest fabric known to man. Or mountain goat.

After all, you've got summits to reach.

So to get more info on the Terraplane and all other Dana Design Packs, drop us a line at 1-800-522-5000.

DANA DESIGN

The realtor said it was perfect.

Spacious, well kept, with a western exposure that's the envy of the neighborhood.

Maybe not.

Dream Home
Or Dutch Oven?

During the summer, a view without Andersen windows turns a perfect home into a perfect oven.

Install Andersen High Performance Sun double pane windows, however, and you've got a unique microscopically thin metallic coating which actually reflects and reduces the sun's heat over two times better than conventional single pane windows.

Technically, they lower the relative heat gain to a comfortable 78 BTU's per square foot per hour. Financially, they save you money. Lots.

The High Performance Sun line also features Andersen's usual strength and durability. Like resistance to winds of at least 155 mph. Hardware tested to 20,000 openings and closings. And water tightness to rival a submarine's.

None of which you need to mention to those who'll stare openly at our classic lines and imaginative shapes.

Just invite them in out of the heat for some lemonade.

After all, no one needs to broil in paradise.

ENGINEERED BY THE MIND FOR THE HEART

We tried to get some of our owners to comment on their watches,
but they couldn't be reached.

ROLEX

ept

Two minutes till reaction time.

(OPPOSITE TOP) 1 STUDENT: REED COSS COLLEGE: PORTFOLIO CENTER, GEORGIA DEGREE: ADVERTISING COUNTRY: USA ■

(OPPOSITE BOTTOM) 2 STUDENT: JOHN PARK COLLEGE: PORTFOLIO CENTER, GEORGIA DEGREE: ADVERTISING COUNTRY: USA ■

(ABOVE LEFT) 3 STUDENT: CHRISTOPHER TURNER COLLEGE: SCHOOL OF VISUAL ARTS DEGREE: ADVERTISING COUNTRY: USA ■

(ABOVE RIGHT) 4 STUDENT: LIZ ADDIS TAYLOR COLLEGE: PORTFOLIO CENTER, GEORGIA DEGREE: ADVERTISING COUNTRY: USA

■ **1** Student: MICHAEL R. CELLA College: SCHOOL OF VISUAL ARTS Degree: BFA Professors: DAVID STERLING, JEFFREY METZNER Country: USA ■ (OPPOSITE PAGE TOP) **2, 3** Student: ARETI VOURAKI College: VAKALO SCHOOL OF ART AND DESIGN Degree: GRAPHIC DESIGN Professor: D. PSOMAS, S. SIMEONIDES Class: 3RD YEAR Country: GREECE ■ (OPPOSITE PAGE BOTTOM) **4, 5** Student: CHRISTOPHER TURNER College: SCHOOL OF VISUAL ARTS Degree: ADVERTISING Professor: JACK MARIUCCI Country: USA

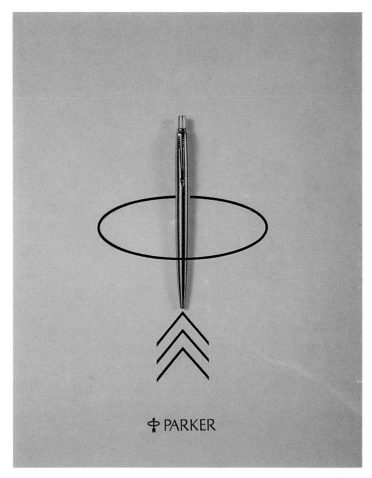

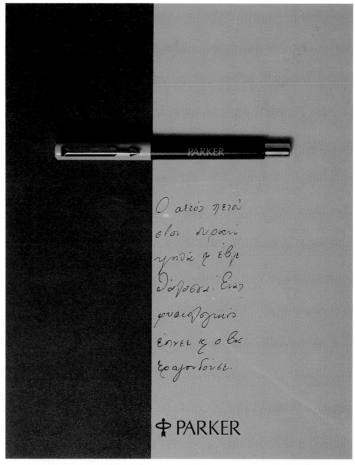

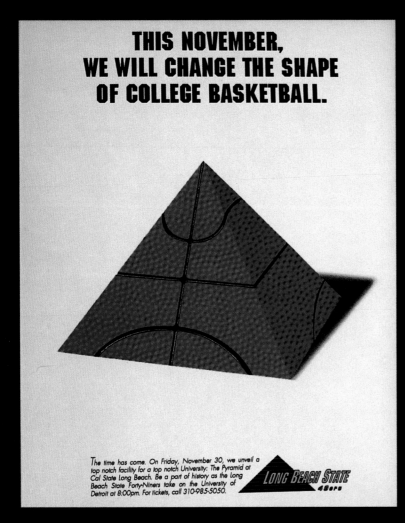

THIS NOVEMBER, WE WILL CHANGE THE SHAPE OF COLLEGE BASKETBALL.

The time has come. On Friday, November 30, we unveil a top notch facility for a top notch University: The Pyramid at Cal State Long Beach. Be a part of history as the Long Beach State Forty-Niners take on the University of Detroit at 8:00pm. For tickets, call 310-985-5050.

LONG BEACH STATE 49ers

AND ON THE EIGHTH DAY, GOD SNIFFED MARKERS.

MEDITERRANEAN IGUANAS $39.
Specializing in the city's coolest reptiles and fish. 666 Java st. Brooklyn. N.Y. (718)DOG MEAT

MARTY'S EXOTIC PETS

■ (THIS PAGE LEFT) **1** STUDENT: DAVE MCCLAIN COLLEGE: CALIFORNIA STATE UNIVERSITY, LONG BEACH DEGREE: BFA PROFESSOR: ARCHIE BOSTON CLASS: ADVERTISING DESIGN COUNTRY: USA ■ (THIS PAGE RIGHT AND OPPOSITE PAGE ALL IMAGES) **2–4** STUDENT: CHRISTOPHER TURNER COLLEGE: SCHOOL OF VISUAL ARTS DEGREE: ADVERTISING PROFESSOR: JACK MARIUCCI COUNTRY: USA

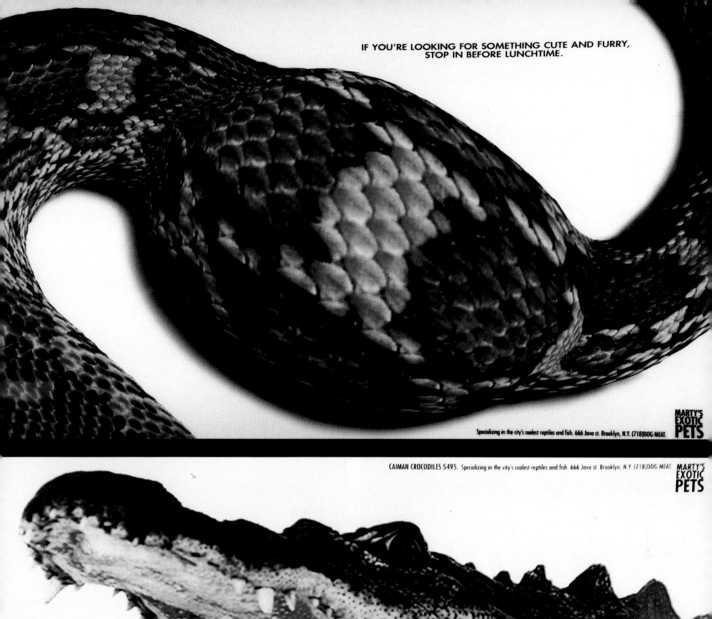

IF YOU'RE LOOKING FOR SOMETHING CUTE AND FURRY,
STOP IN BEFORE LUNCHTIME.

Specializing in the city's coolest reptiles and fish. 666 Java st. Brooklyn, N.Y. (718)DOG-MEAT.

MARTY'S
EXOTIC
PETS

CAIMAN CROCODILES $495. Specializing in the city's coolest reptiles and fish. 666 Java st. Brooklyn, N.Y. (718)DOG-MEAT.

MARTY'S
EXOTIC
PETS

SURE IT'LL CATCH A FRISBEE,
IF YOU TIE A POODLE TO IT.

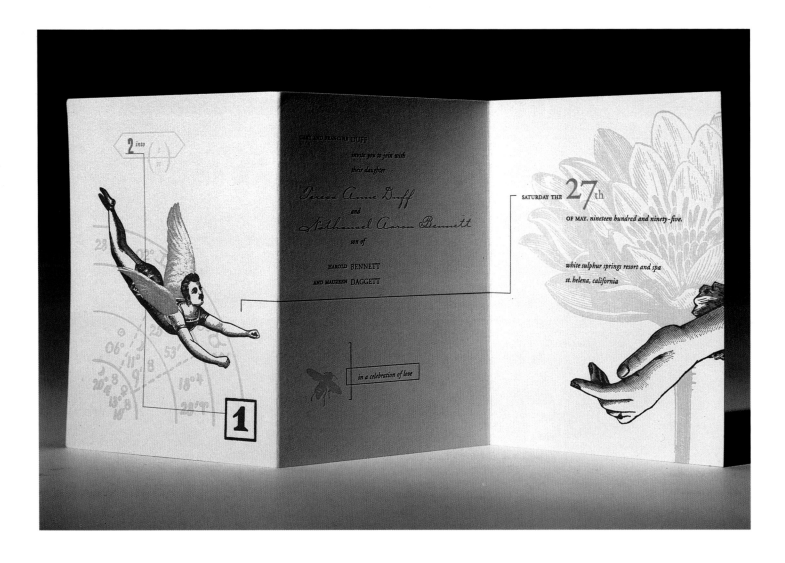

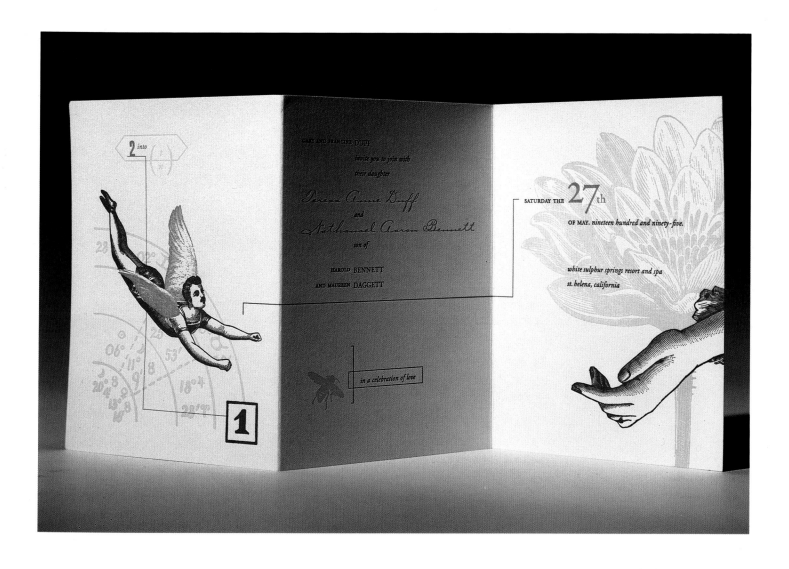

■ (ABOVE) **1** STUDENT: GABY BRINK COLLEGE: CALIFORNIA COLLEGE OF ARTS & CRAFTS DEGREE: BFA IN GRAPHIC DESIGN COUNTRY: USA ■ (OPPOSITE PAGE) **2, 3** STUDENT: MILER HUNG COLLEGE: TEXAS CHRISTIAN UNIVERSITY CLASS: INDIVIDUAL STUDY COUNTRY: USA

Born

tu

bi

Schrift

: von Shop.

Schie lawws ju Schrift

: von Shop.

Bäibi jukän dreifmei Schrift

: von Shop.

Ohlju nied is Schrift

: *von Shop.*

Ei kahnt getno Schrift

: von Shop.

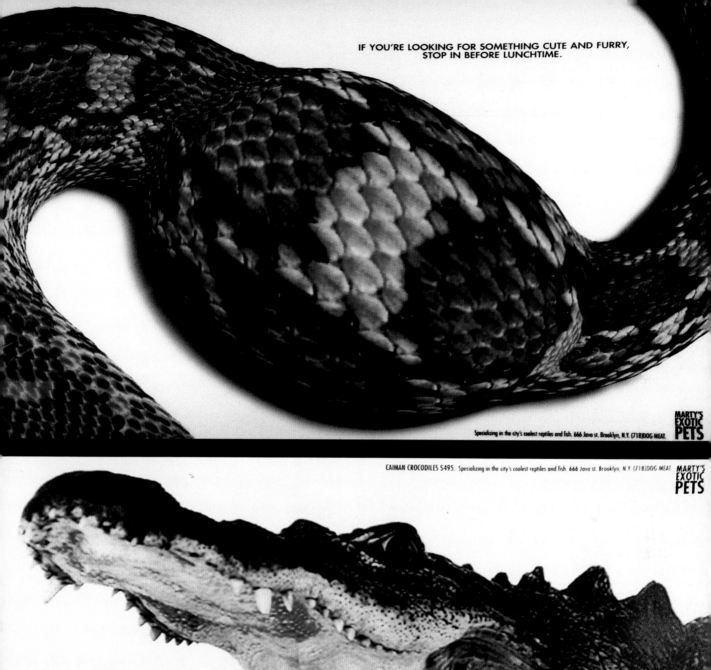

IF YOU'RE LOOKING FOR SOMETHING CUTE AND FURRY,
STOP IN BEFORE LUNCHTIME.

Specializing in the city's coolest reptiles and fish. 666 Java st. Brooklyn, N.Y. (718)DOG-MEAT.

MARTY'S
EXOTIC
PETS

CAIMAN CROCODILES $495. Specializing in the city's coolest reptiles and fish. 666 Java st. Brooklyn, N.Y. (718)DOG-MEAT.

MARTY'S
EXOTIC
PETS

SURE IT'LL CATCH A FRISBEE,
IF YOU TIE A POODLE TO IT.

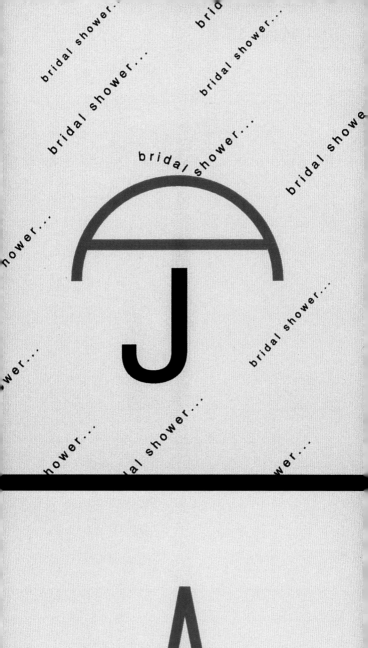

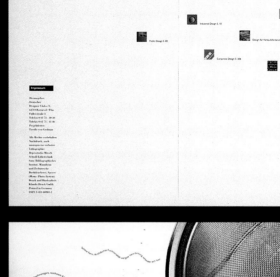

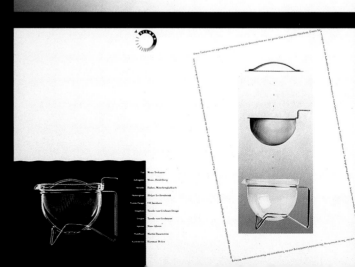

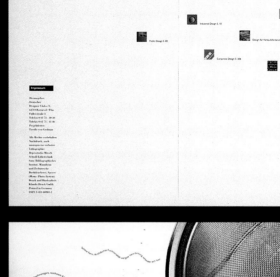

Was hat das deutsche Design wirklich zu bieten?
Deutscher Designer Club · Auszeichnung 1991

Teilnahme-Coupon

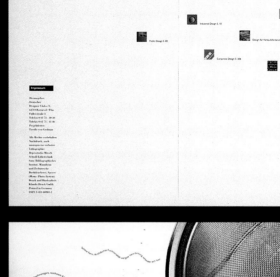

INHALT

Industrial Design S. 10
Grafik-Design S. 67
Public Design S. 89
Design für Verkaufsförderung S. 124
Mode- und Trend-Design S. 161
Corporate Design S. 206
System-Design S. 234

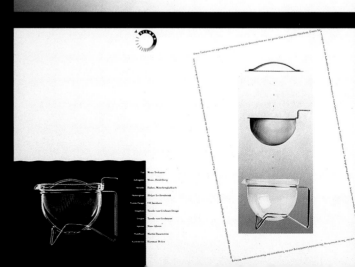

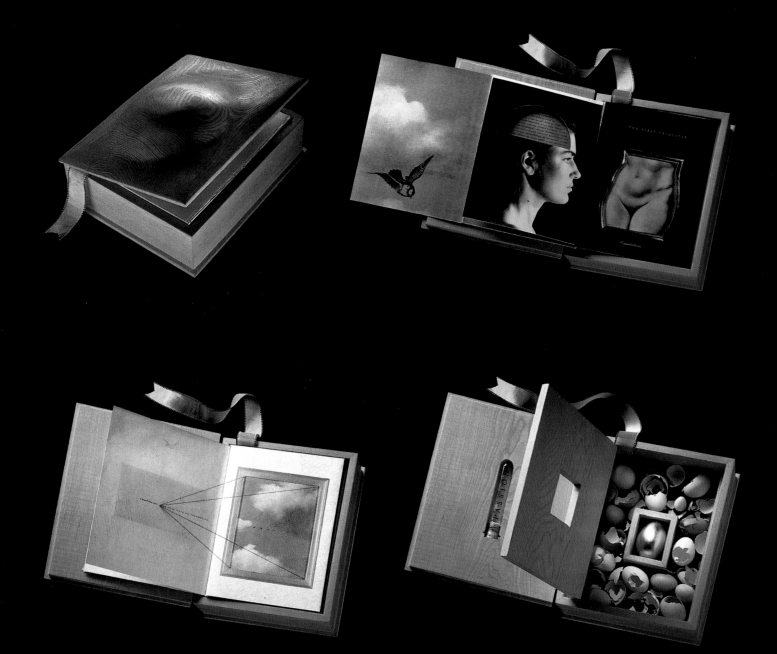

(THIS SPREAD)
STUDENT: JENNIFER JERDE
COLLEGE: CALIFORNIA COLLEGE OF ARTS & CRAFTS
DEGREE: BFA
PROFESSOR: MICHAEL VANDERBYL
COUNTRY: USA

The reward of labor is life.

WILLIAM MORRIS

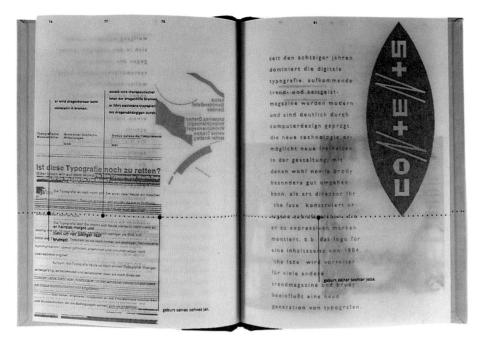

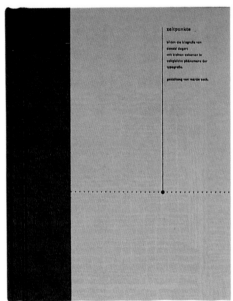

■ (OPPOSITE PAGE) **1–3** Student: MARTIN ZECH College: HOCHSCHULE FÜR KÜNSTE BREMEN Degree: GRAPHIC DESIGN (DIPLOM GRAPHIK DESIGNER) Professor: VICTOR MALSY Class: BASIC COURSE TYPOGRAPHY Country: GERMANY ■ **4** (THIS PAGE) Student: MERLIN LEMBONG College: CALIFORNIA COLLEGE OF ARTS & CRAFTS Degree: BFA Professor: MICHAEL VANDERBYL Country: USA

■ (THIS PAGE) **1** Student: LYNNE PEKAREK College: IOWA STATE UNIVERSITY Degree: BFA, GRAPHIC DESIGN Professor: ROGER BAER Class: INDEPENDENT STUDY Country: USA ■ (OPPOSITE PAGE) **2–9** Student: LARS CHRISTENSEN College: KUNSTHAAND-VAERKERSKOLEN KOLDING Degree: MA, ILLUSTRATION Professor: H.C. NEDABROWSKY Class: 5TH YEAR Country: DENMARK

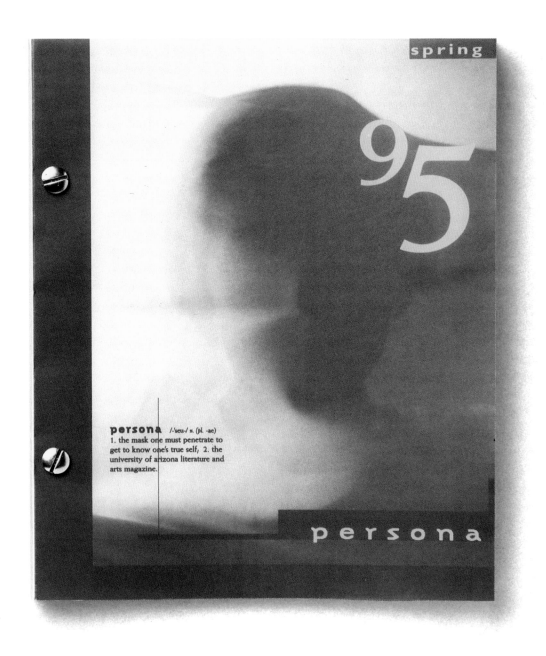

■ **1** STUDENTS: VALERIE ROABERG, GEOFF LEDET COLLEGE: UNIVERSITY OF ARIZONA DEGREE: BFA IN GRAPHIC DESIGN ART DIRECTOR: ELLEN MCMAHON COUNTRY: USA ■ (OPPOSITE) **2, 3** STUDENT: LUTZ EBERLE COLLEGE: STAATLICHE AKADEMIE DER BILDENDEN KÜNSTE STUTTGART DEGREE: GRAPHIC DESIGN PROFESSORS: GÜNTER JACKI, MANFRED KRÖPLIEN CLASS: 9TH TERM COUNTRY: GERMANY

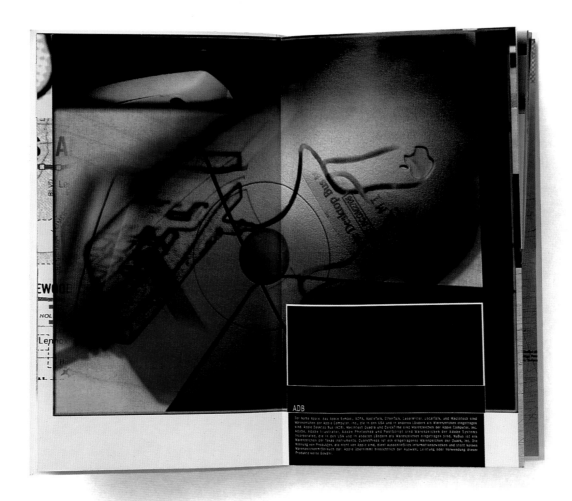

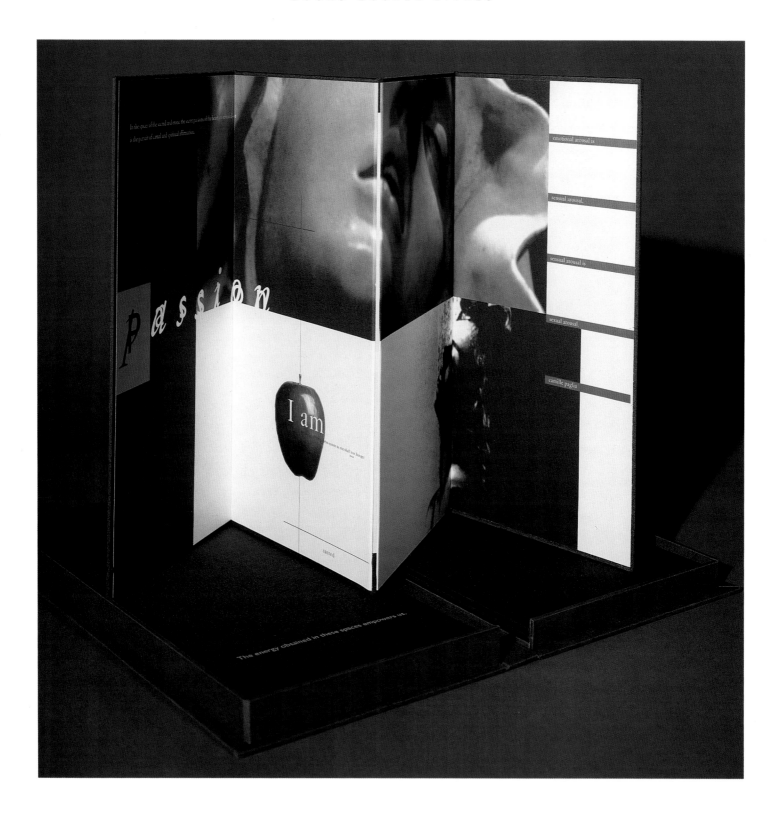

■ **1** STUDENT: PAIGE STUART COLLEGE: CALIFORNIA COLLEGE OF ARTS & CRAFTS DEGREE: BFA, DESIGN PROFESSOR: MICHAEL VANDERBYL COUNTRY: USA ■ **2, 5** STUDENT: LUTZ WIDMAIER COLLEGE: STAATLICHE AKADEMIE DER BILDENDEN KÜNSTE STUTTGART DEGREE: GRAPHIC DESIGN PROFESSOR: HEINZ EDELMANN CLASS: 5TH YEAR COUNTRY: GERMANY ■ **3** STUDENT: DIMITRIOS KRITSOTAKIS COLLEGE: VAKALO SCHOOL OF ART AND DESIGN DEGREE: GRAPHIC DESIGN PROFESSOR: H. HARALAMBOUS CLASS: 3RD YEAR COUNTRY: GREECE ■ **4** STUDENT: MILER HUNG COLLEGE: TEXAS CHRISTIAN UNIVERSITY PROFESSOR: MARGIE ADKINS CLASS: GRAPHIC III COUNTRY: USA

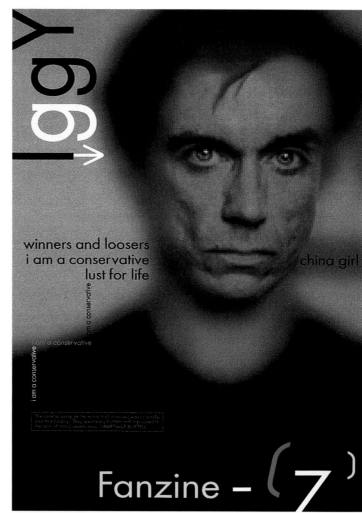

FISCHER

EINHORN

SPHINX UND

SALAMANDER

JORGE LUIS

BORGES

■ 1 STUDENT: PÉTER VAJDA COLLEGE: HUNGARIAN ACADEMY OF FINE ARTS DEGREE: GRAPHIC DESIGN PROFESSORS: GYÖRGY OLÁH (GRAPHIC DESIGN), ATTILA AUTH (TYPOGRAPHY) CLASS: 2ND YEAR COUNTRY: HUNGARY ■ 2 STUDENT: HEATHER DEGA COLLEGE:

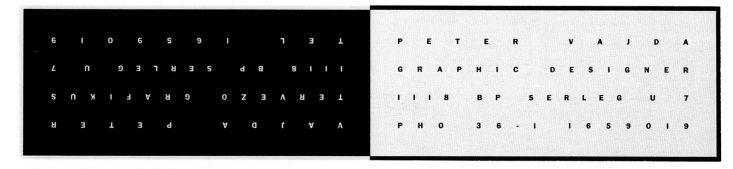

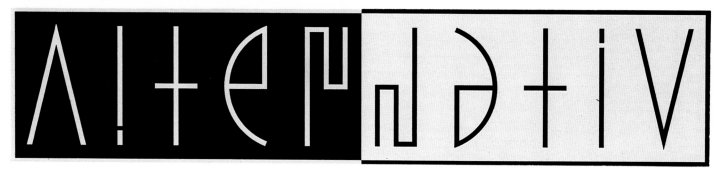

SCHOOL OF VISUAL ARTS DEGREE: BFA, GRAPHIC DESIGN COUNTRY: USA ■ 3 STUDENT: WOLFGANG GRETER COLLEGE: FACHHOCH-SCHULE FÜR GESTALTUNG AUGSBURG DEGREE: GRAPHIC DESIGN PROFESSOR: RAINER FROST CLASS: 9TH TERM COUNTRY: GERMANY

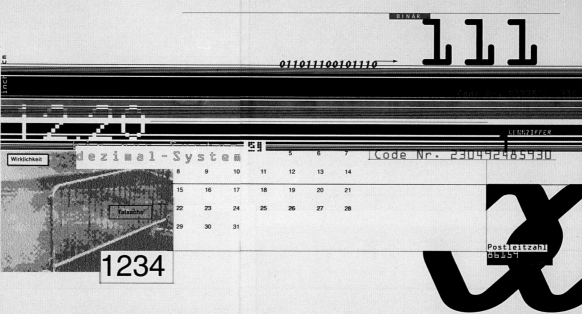

Definition

Eine Definition ist keine Manifestation der Natur, sondern stets nur ein Werkzeug, das uns bei der Erreichung unserer Zwecke behilflich ist.

I.A. Richards: Wir wollen etwas tun, und eine Definition ist ein Mittel, um es zu tun. Wenn wir bestimmte Ergebnisse wollen, müssen wir bestimmte Definitionen verwenden. Aber unabhängig von einem Zweck kommt keiner Definition irgendeine Autorität zu, auch nicht die Autorität, uns andere Zwecksetzungen zu verbieten. Man sollte den Menschen deutlich machen, daß Definitionen nicht von Gott gegeben sind; daß wir von ihnen abweichen dürfen, ohne unser Seelenheil aufs Spiel zu setzen; daß die Autorität einer Definition ganz und gar auf ihrer Nützlichkeit beruht und nicht auf ihrer Richtigkeit (was immer das bedeuten würde); daß es ein Ausdruck von Dummheit ist, wenn man einem anderen dessen Definition eines Wortes, eines Problems oder einer Situation ohne Überlegung abnimmt. Und schließlich, daß dies alles für die Definition eines Wortes oder Moleküls genauso gilt wie für eine Definition.

Neil Postman
Die Verweigerung der Hörigkeit

BINAR

01101110010111O →

111

Code Nr. ?????? ????

KENNZIFFER

Wirklichkeit

dezimal-System

						5	6	7

Code Nr. 230442485930

	8	9	10	11	12	13	14
	15	16	17	18	19	20	21
Tatsache	22	23	24	25	26	27	28
	29	30	31				

1234

Postleitzahl
86154

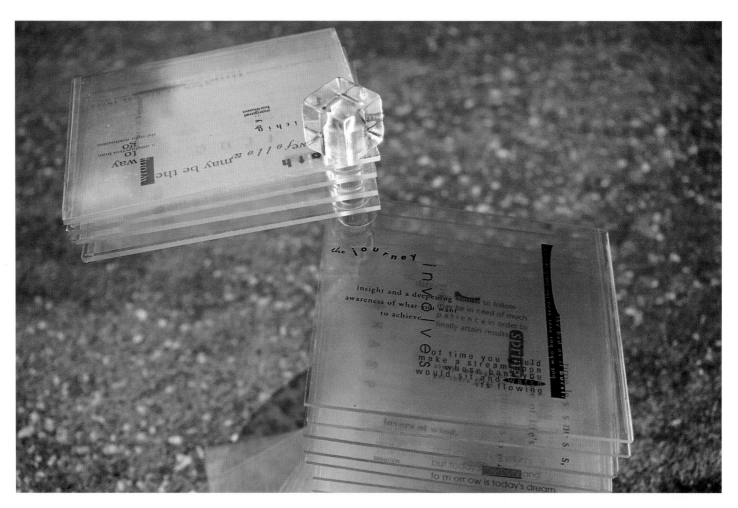

Three Cash Dollars

Three dollars cash
For a pair of catalog shoes
Was what the midwife charged
My mama
For bringing me.
"We wasn't so country then," says Mom,
"You being the last one—
And we couldn't, like
We done
When she brought your
Brother,
Send her out to the
Pen
And let her pick
Out
A pig."

selected poems by Alice Walker

■ (OPPOSITE PAGE) **1, 2** STUDENT: MARGARET A. HARTMANN COLLEGE: UNIVERSITY OF FLORIDA DEGREE: BFA PROFESSORS: MUNEERA UMEDALY, SPENCE KARMAL COUNTRY: USA ■ (THIS PAGE) **3** STUDENT: PATRICIA EVANGELISTA COLLEGE: CALIFORNIA COLLEGE OF ARTS & CRAFTS DEGREE: GRAPHIC DESIGN PROFESSOR: BOB AUFULDISH CLASS: GRAPHIC DESIGN II COUNTRY: USA

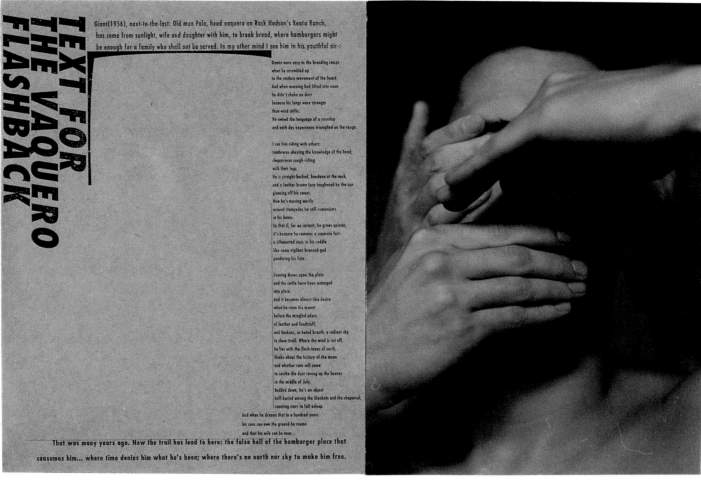

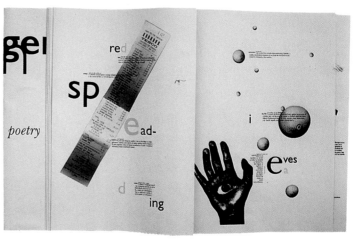

(OPPOSITE PAGE, TOP AND BOTTOM ROW) **1, 2, 4, 5** STUDENT: PETER PARKER COLLEGE: COLCHESTER INSTITUTE DEGREE: BA PROFESSOR: DAVID JURY CLASS: 3RD YEAR COUNTRY: GREAT BRITAIN ■ (OPPOSITE PAGE, CENTER) **3** STUDENT: BENJAMIN PHAM COLLEGE: CALIFORNIA COLLEGE OF ARTS & CRAFTS DEGREE: BA OF GRAPHIC DESIGN CLASS: GRAPHIC DESIGN 2 COUNTRY: USA

■ **6** (THIS PAGE) STUDENT: DEREK THOMPSON COLLEGE: ILLINOIS STATE UNIVERSITY DEGREE: BS IN GRAPHIC DESIGN PROFESSOR: PAMELA TANNURA CLASS: GRAPHIC DESIGN 4 COUNTRY: USA ■ (FOLLOWING SPREAD ALL IMAGES) **1–3** STUDENT: MONIKA KASZTA COLLEGE: HUNGARIAN ACADEMY OF CRAFTS AND DESIGN DEGREE: ILLUSTRATION CLASS: 3RD YEAR COUNTRY: HUNGARY

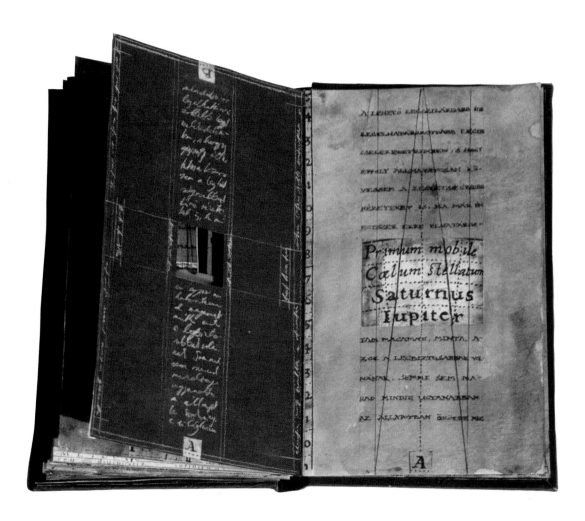

Industrial Revolution

ADVANCED CONCEPT DESIGN STUDY OF A COMPUTER WORKSTATION BY JONAS H BOURGHARDT

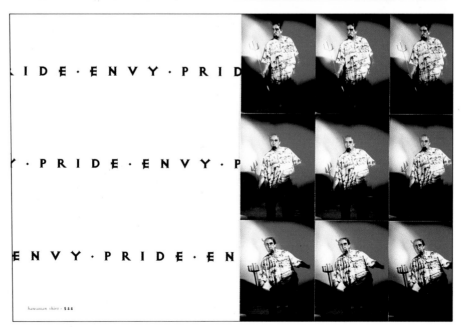

willkommen zu unserem neuen
besteck - Programm
edition zero
das komplette besteck sowie das
geschirr besteht aus porzellan und

emaille.
beständigkeit und schönheit sind
unser credo.

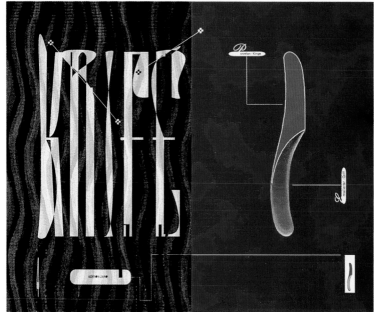

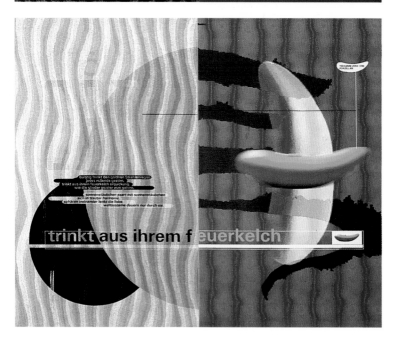

(PRECEDING SPREAD LEFT) **1** STUDENT: JONAS BOURGHARDT COLLEGE: ART CENTER EUROPE DEGREE: B.SC. PRODUCT DESIGN COUNTRY: SWITZERLAND ■ (PRECEDING SPREAD RIGHT) **2–4** STUDENTS: GARTH DAVIS, DAVID TREWERN, CHRIS TSERNJAVSKI COLLEGE: THE

SWINBURNE SCHOOL OF DESIGN DEGREE: BA, GRAPHIC DESIGN PROFESSOR: ANDREW HAIG COUNTRY: AUSTRALIA ■ (THIS SPREAD) STUDENT: STEFAN ROEDEL COLLEGE: BLOCHERER SCHULE DEGREE: GRAPHIC DESIGN PROFESSOR: KLAUS MÜLLER CLASS: 7TH TERM COUNTRY: GERMANY

WHY STUDY PHOTOGRAPHY AT RINGLING?

Ringling School is a four-year college of professional visual arts. That means you will live and work in a diverse community of students and faculty who share a visual language and a strong commitment to art and design. All students begin with Foundation Studies, a yearlong curriculum of drawing and design courses that provides a working knowledge of the principles common to all the visual arts. This multidisciplinary approach continues in your sophomore year as you have the opportunity to supplement your studies in photography with electives from the Departments of Computer Animation, Fine Arts, Graphic Design and Illustration.

The Department of Photography prepares its students to utilize the camera as a tool to communicate practical and expressive ideas. As a photography major you will learn lighting, camera, darkroom and electronic-imaging techniques. You will develop the traditional, conceptual and technological skills that serve as the foundation for both fine art and commercial applications. A Ringling education in the Department of Photography will allow you to follow your vision to a lifetime of personal and professional achievement.

"I LIKE TO USE THE PHOTOGRAPHIC
PROCESS AS A WAY OF WALKING THE PATH
BETWEEN IMPRESSION AND EXPRESSION, THE
UNDEFINED AND THE EXACT. I HOPE THAT
MY IMAGES CAN, IN SOME WAY, SENSUOUSLY
RENEW THE APPEARANCE OF THINGS TO
HUMAN EYES." THOMAS CARABASI, FACULTY

JIM ATWELL

MICHAEL LONG

(THIS SPREAD)
STUDENTS: JODY HANEKE, MICHAEL LONG
COLLEGE: RINGLING SCHOOL OF ART AND DESIGN
DEGREE: BFA IN GRAPHIC DESIGN
PROFESSOR: JENNIFER MUMFORD
CLASS: DESIGN CENTER
COUNTRY: USA

Creativität

In Skandinavien werden die Bürozellen im allgemeinen durch eine deckenmontierte Leuchtstofflampe im Arbeitsbereich und eine zusätzlich abgependelte Rundleuchte am Besprechungstisch ausgeleuchtet. Die Lichtverteilung hierzu läßt sich schematisch in Abbildung 8 erkennen. Die Leuchtdichte einer derartigen Anordnung reicht häufig auf den Arbeistflächen, die an den Wänden entlang angeordent sind, nicht mehr aus, so daß in der Regel zusätzlich ein bis zwei Arbeitsplatzleuchten installiert werden müssen. Um ein besseres Lichtmilieu zu erhalten, hat es sich daher meist als sinnvoller erwiesen, den Raum insgesamt indierekt zu beleuchten, so daß eine Raumnbeleuchtungstärke mit etwa 200 bis 300 Lux erreicht wird. Ergänzend hierzu erhält der Schreibtisch ein Arbetsleuchte von circa 500 bis 700 Lux im Arbeitsbereich.

Beleuchtung

Aufgrund der flexiblen Nutzung der Multiräume bietet sich eine indirekte Beleuchtung als ideale Lösung an. Hierdurch kann eine ausreichende Allgemeinbeleuchtung mit circa 200 bis 300 Lux Beleuchtungsstärke erreicht werden, und im Einzelfall sind, je nach Nutzungscharakter, zusätzliche Arbeitsplatz- oder Besprechungstischbeleuchtungen hinzuzufügen. Das Schema in Abbildung 13 zeigt eine deckeninstallierte Indierktbeleuchung. Bei Verwendung Hohlraum- oder Doppelbodens ist es ohne weiteres möglich, eine flexible indirekte Beleuchtung durch Stehleuchten zu erreichen, um die flexible Ausstattung des Multiraums weiter zu erhöhen.

(THIS SPREAD)

STUDENT: STEFAN ROEDEL

COLLEGE: BLOCHERER SCHULE

DEGREE: GRAPHIC DESIGN

PROFESSOR: KLAUS MÜLLER

CLASS: 7. SEMESTER

COUNTRY: GERMANY

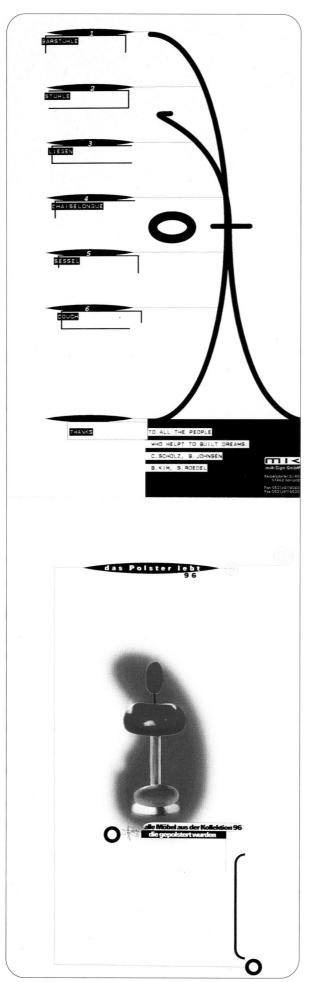

1 BARSTÜHLE

2 STÜHLE

3 LIEGEN

4 CHAISELONGUE

5 SESSEL

6 COUCH

THANKS TO ALL THE PEOPLE
WHO HELPT TO BUILT DREAMS.
C. SCHOLZ, B. JOHNSEN
B. KIM, S. ROEDEL

mik
mik-Sign GmbH
Kesselsdorfer Str. 40
01462 Gompitz
Fon 0531/4114040
Fax 0531/4116530

das Polster lebt
96

alle Möbel aus der Kollektion 96
die gepolstert wurden

Modell Pianno
250 31-6

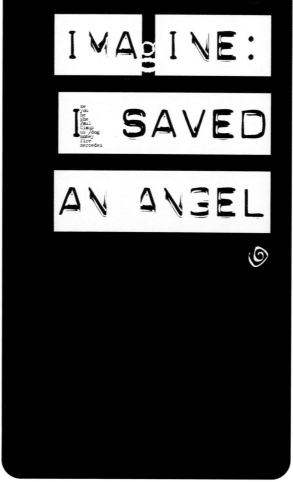

IMAGINE:

me
you
he
Rüm
Paul
Claus
us /dog
money
fire
mercedes

I SAVED

AN ANGEL

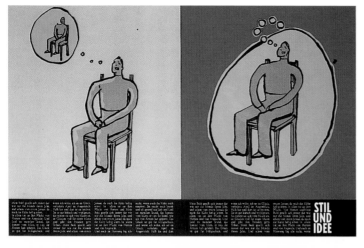

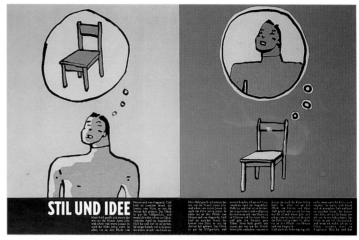

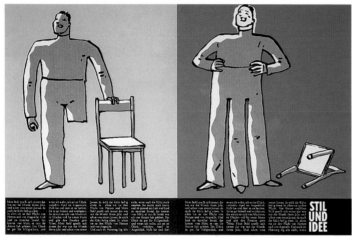

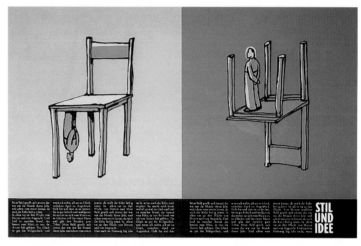

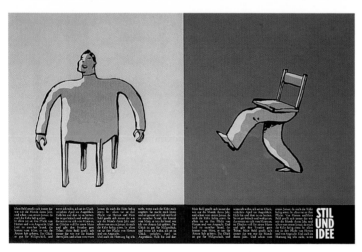

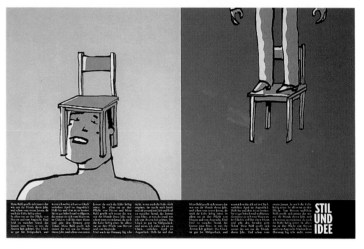

■ (THIS PAGE) 1–6 STUDENT: CHRISTOPH NIEMANN COLLEGE: STAATLICHE AKADEMIE DER BILDENDEN KÜNSTE STUTTGART
DEGREE: GRAPHIC DESIGN PROFESSOR: HEINZ EDELMANN CLASS: 4TH YEAR COUNTRY: GERMANY ■ (OPPOSITE PAGE) 7
STUDENT: GABY BRINK COLLEGE: CALIFORNIA COLLEGE OF ARTS & CRAFTS DEGREE: BFA IN GRAPHIC DESIGN COUNTRY: USA

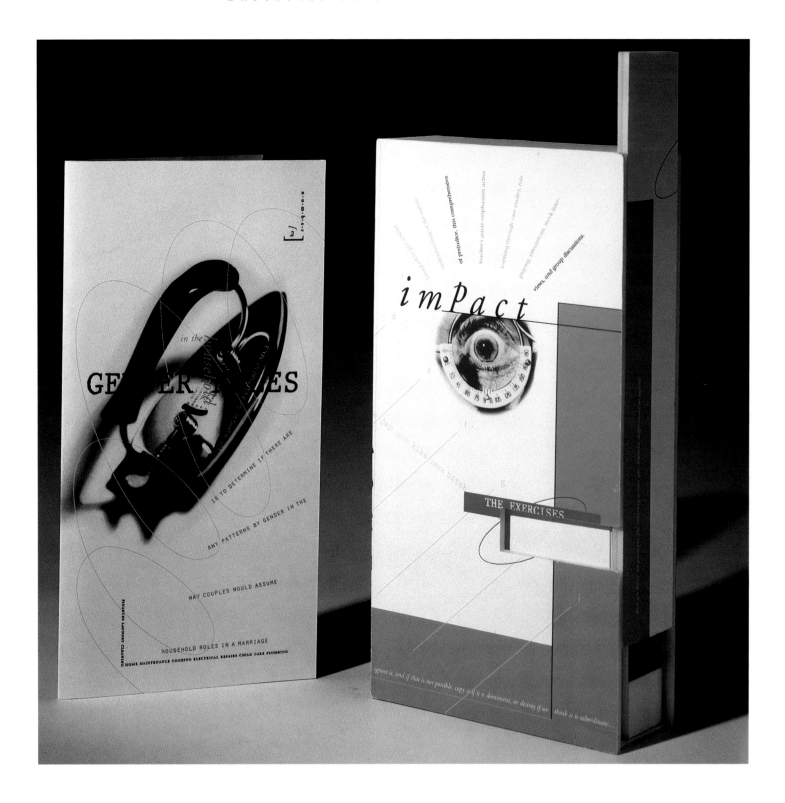

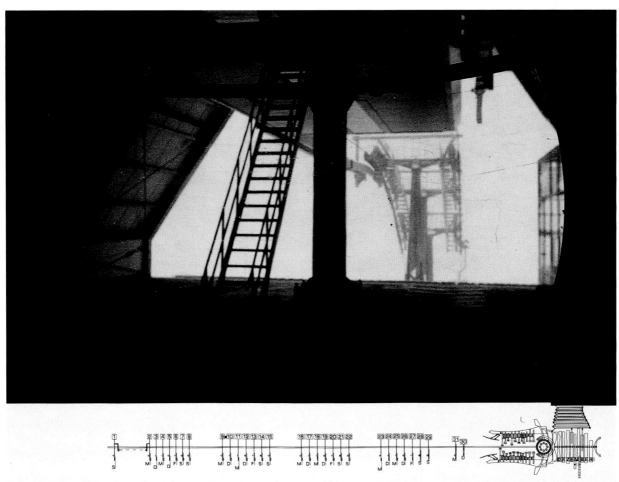

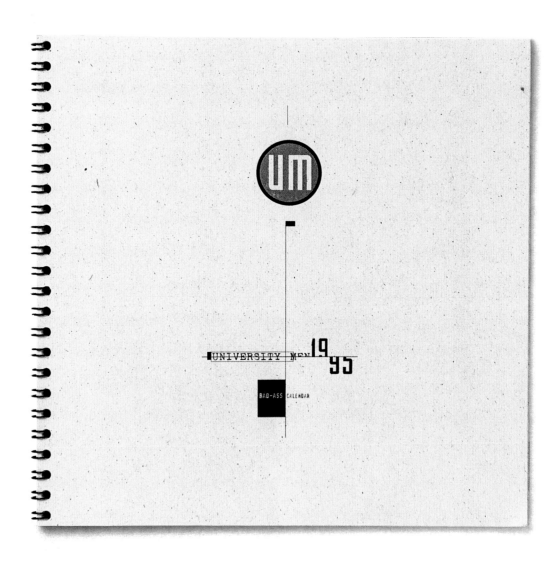

(PRECEDING SPREAD) **1–4** STUDENT: DAMIAN HEINISCH COLLEGE: UNIVERSITÄT GH ESSEN DEGREE: COMMUNICATION DESIGN PROFESSORS: VOLKER KÜSTER (TYPOGRAPHY), INGE OSSWALD AND ERICH VOM ENDT (PHOTOGRAPHY) CLASS: 8TH TERM COUNTRY: GERMANY ■ (THIS SPREAD) **1–4** STUDENTS: PATRICK BOSAK (DESIGN), ASHTON WORTHINGTON (PHOTOGRAPHY) COLLEGE: UNIVERSITY OF DELAWARE DEGREE: BS IN VISUAL COMMUNICATION PROFESSORS: MARTHA CAROTHERS, RAY NICHOLS COUNTRY: USA ■ (FOLLOWING SPREAD) **1–8** STUDENT: STEFANIE HALBACH COLLEGE: BERGISCHE UNIVERSITÄT WUPPERTAL DEGREE: COMMUNICATION DESIGN PROFESSOR: UWE LOESCH COUNTRY: GERMANY

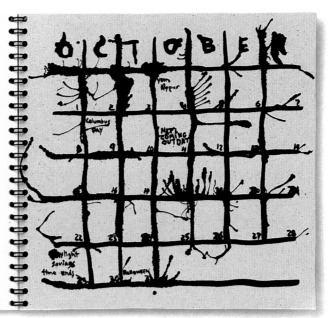

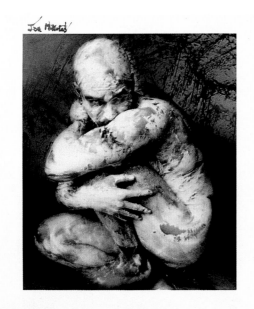

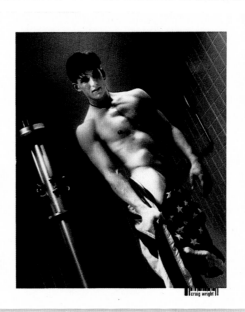

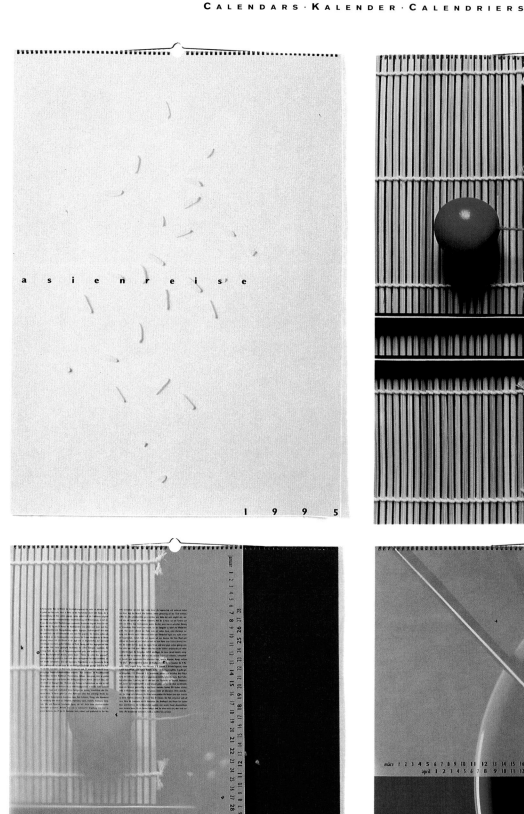

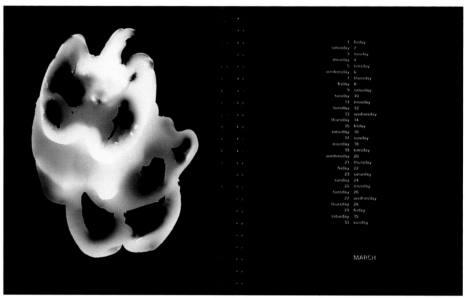

■ (ABOVE) **1, 2** S TUDENT: ELLEN KYUNG KIM C OLLEGE: PENN STATE UNIVERSITY D EGREE: GRAPHIC DESIGN P ROFESSORS: LANNY SOMMESE, KRISTIN BRESLIN SOMMESE C OUNTRY: USA ■ (OPPOSITE) **3–10** S TUDENT: DEBORAH HANUSA C OLLEGE: FACHHOCHSCHULE RHEINLAND-PFALZ, ABT. MAINZ 1 D EGREE: CORPORATE DESIGN P ROFESSOR: OLAF LEU C LASS: GRADUATE THESIS C OUNTRY: GERMANY

heine.
Die Welt des Besonderen

heine.
Die Welt des Besonderen

heine.

heine.

helline.

HAUPTKATALOG
HERBST/WINTER 1994/95

heine.

MODE AMBIENTE ACCESSOIRES

heine.

heine.

heine.

heine

(THIS SPREAD)

STUDENT: HARDY LAHN

COLLEGE: FACHHOCHSCHULE RHEINLAND-PFALZ, ABT. MAINZ 1

DEGREE: CORPORATE DESIGN

PROFESSOR: OLAF LEU

CLASS: GRADUATE THESIS

COUNTRY: GERMANY

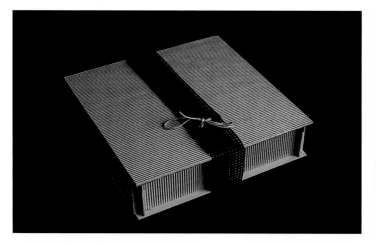

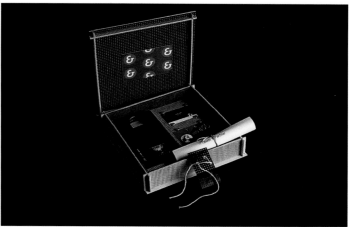

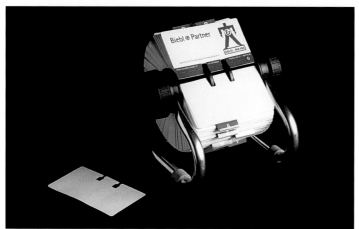

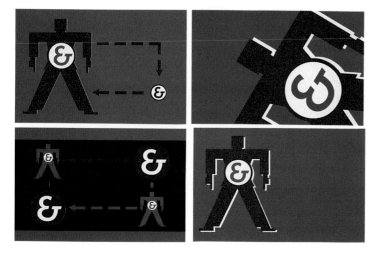

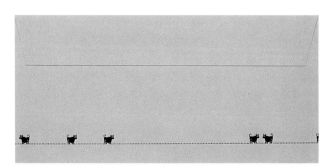

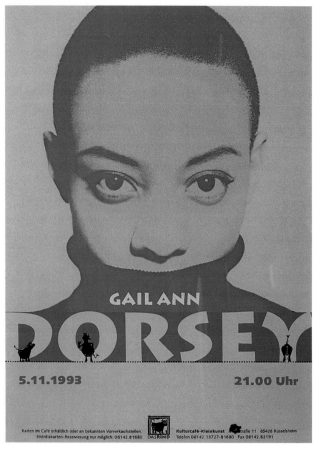

STUDENT: KERSTIN MINDERMANN

COLLEGE: FACHHOCHSCHULE RHEINLAND-PFALZ, ABT. MAINZ 1

DEGREE: CORPORATE DESIGN

PROFESSOR: OLAF LEU

CLASS: GRADUATE THESIS

COUNTRY: GERMANY

Cu
cobre

Mn
manganeso

Zn
zinc

Ag
plata

Fe
hierro

mercurio

Hg

plomo

Pb

platino

Pt

tungsteno

W

oro

Au

DIRECTOR

PRESIDENTE

GERENTE GENERAL

BANCO CENTRAL DE RESERVA DEL PERU

LITERATURA

Ciro Alegría José María Arguedas Carlos Gérma
Belli José Santos Chocano Antonio Cisneros Isa
Goldemberg Manuel Gonzáles Prada Gui
Gutiérrez Merino Javier Héraud César M
Sebastián Salazar Bondy Nicomedes Santa C
Manuel Scorza César Vallejo Mario Vargas Llos

A2753680B

10

NUEVOS SOLES

BANCO CENTRAL DE RESERVA DEL PERU

A la libertad

Por fin libre y seguro
puedo cantar. Rompióse el duro freno,
descubriré mi seno,
y con lenguaje puro
mostraré la verdad que en él se anida,
mi libertad civil entendida.

Textiles Incas

10

10

DIEZ   NUEVOS SOLES

La Serpiente, símbolo del conocimiento y la inteligencia

10

■ (OPPOSITE) **1, 2** STUDENT: RAFAEL ESQUER COLLEGE: ART CENTER COLLEGE OF DESIGN DEGREE: GRAPHICS AND PACKAGING DESIGN MAJOR PROFESSOR: REBECA MÉNDEZ CLASS: TYPOGRAPHY I COUNTRY: USA ■ (ABOVE) **3** STUDENT: DAVID TREWERN COLLEGE: THE SWINBURNE SCHOOL OF DESIGN DEGREE: BACHELOR OF DESIGN IN GRAPHIC DESIGN LECTURER: ANDREW HAIG COUNTRY: AUSTRALIA

JANUARY 1995 S12

PICTURE

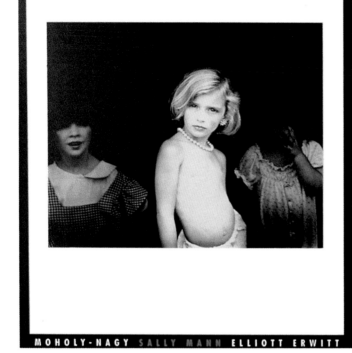

MOHOLY-NAGY SALLY MANN ELLIOTT ERWITT

JANUARY 1995 S12

PICTURE

MOHOLY-NAGY ELLIOTT ERWITT SALLY MANN

(THIS SPREAD)

STUDENT: MONICA SIN-HAN CHIU

COLLEGE: SCHOOL OF VISUAL ARTS

DEGREE: BFA

PROFESSOR: CARIN GOLDBERG

CLASS: SENIOR PORTFOLIO

COUNTRY: USA

visual
p u n
Eliotts
through
Erwitt
camera

Erwitt's art is

(tender)

without crying,

[funny]

without laughing,

{intellingent}

without thinking.

NEW YORK 1976

RICH
A
D

R

Richard Avedon has been a restless and relentless chronicer of our time. One has given a nation a more widenegth

AVEDON

Replace of the fashion year he put an autobiography foiling year collaboead with Jame

THE POWER OF

SUND

Dolor in hendrerit in vulputate velit esse molestie consequat, vel illum dolore eu feugiat nulla facilisis at vero eros et accumsan et iusto odio dignissim qui blandit praesent luptatum zzril delenit augue duis dolore te feugait nulla facilisi diam nonummy. Ut wisi enim ad minim veniam, quis nostrud exerci tation

Lorem ipsum dolor sit amet, con sectetuer adipiscing elit, sed diam nonummy nibh euismod tincidunt ut laoreet dolore magna aliquam erat volutpat. Ut wisi enim ad minim veniam, quis nostrud exerci tation ullam corper suscipit lobortis nisl ut aliquip ex ea commodo consequat. Duis aute veleum iriure dolor in hendrerit in vulputate velit esse molestie consequat. Vel illum.

Dolore eu feuglat nulla facilisis at vero eros et accumsan et iusto odio dignissim qui blandit praesent luptatum zzril delenit augue duis dolore te feugait nulla facilisi. Lorem ipsum dolor sit amet, con sectetuer adipiscing elit, sed diam nonummy nibh euismod tincidunt ut laoreet dolore magna aliquam erat volutpat. Ut wisi enim ad minim veniam. Nostrud exerci. Katusu tillamcorper sus cipit lobortis nisl ut aliquip ex ea commodo consequat. Autem vel eum iriure.

MY WORK HAS NO AESTHETIC VALUES OTHER THAN THE AESTHETIC OF COMMUNICATION.

I BELIEVE ARTISTS MUST EXPLOIT THEMSELVES. THEY MUST TAKE THE RISK AND THE LOT ELSE THE VIEWERS.

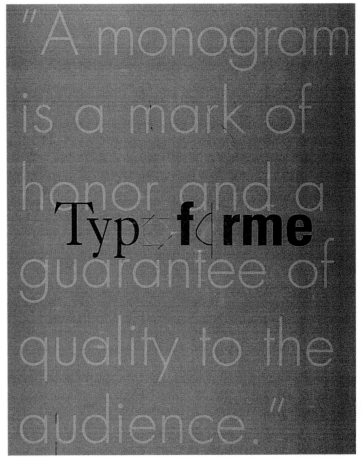

"A monogram is a mark of honor and a guarantee of quality to the audience."

Typ forme

Belgacom

INFO

maart nr. 2

JOURNAL

THE NEWS MAGAZINE

volume 53 $2.95 december 14, 1994

ANNETTE

HER LIFE
WITH DRUGS
AND AIDS

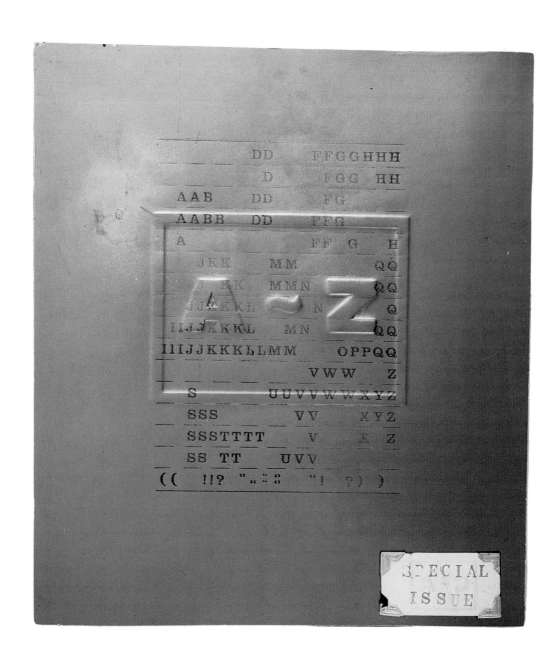

(THIS PAGE) **1** STUDENT: DAVID BYUN COLLEGE: SCHOOL OF VISUAL ARTS DEGREE: BFA, GRAPHIC DESIGN PROFESSOR: CHIP KIDD COUNTRY: USA ■ (OPPOSITE PAGE) **2–4** STUDENT: EFRAT RAFAELI COLLEGE: SCHOOL OF VISUAL ARTS DEGREE: BFA PROFESSORS: CHRIS AUSTOPCHUCK, CHIP KIDD, BARBARA DE WILDE COUNTRY: USA ■ (FOLLOWING SPREAD, ALL IMAGES) **1–5** STUDENT: JAN FEDERMANN (WINNER OF THE GOLD MEDAL IN THE 7TH INTERNATIONAL DESIGN COMPETITION OSAKA 1995) COLLEGE: BERGISCHE UNIVERSITÄT WUPPERTAL DEGREE: COMMUNICATION DESIGN PROFESSOR: UWE LOESCH COUNTRY: GERMANY

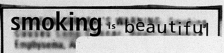

smoking is beautiful

The media make believe.

I'll make you sexy. I'll make you skinny. I'll make you pretty. I'll make you COOL

the REASONS and the RESULTS.

by Efrat Razeli. Photo: Irving Penn

PHENOMENON

iT looks So cool It Makes me

Puke.

fashion and **B**ulimia

photographer: Steven Meisel
by efrat razeli

THING

This page: Silver Lace and silver beads bra, about $2000 at Channel. (Photography: Albert watson.)

watchout

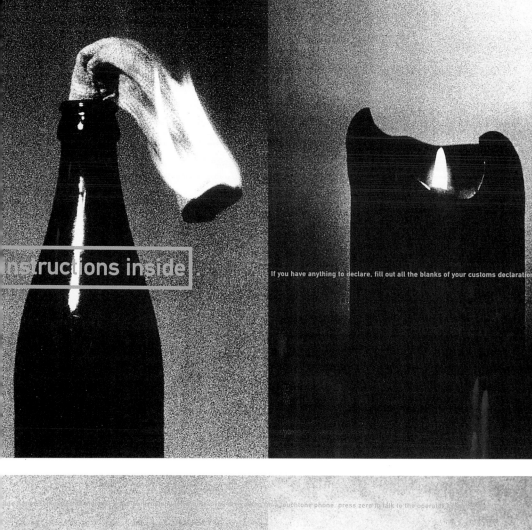

instructions inside.

If you have anything to declare, fill out all the blanks of your customs declaration

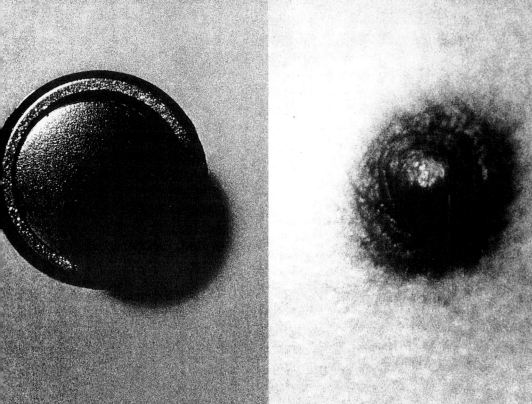

touchtone phone, press zero to talk to the operator

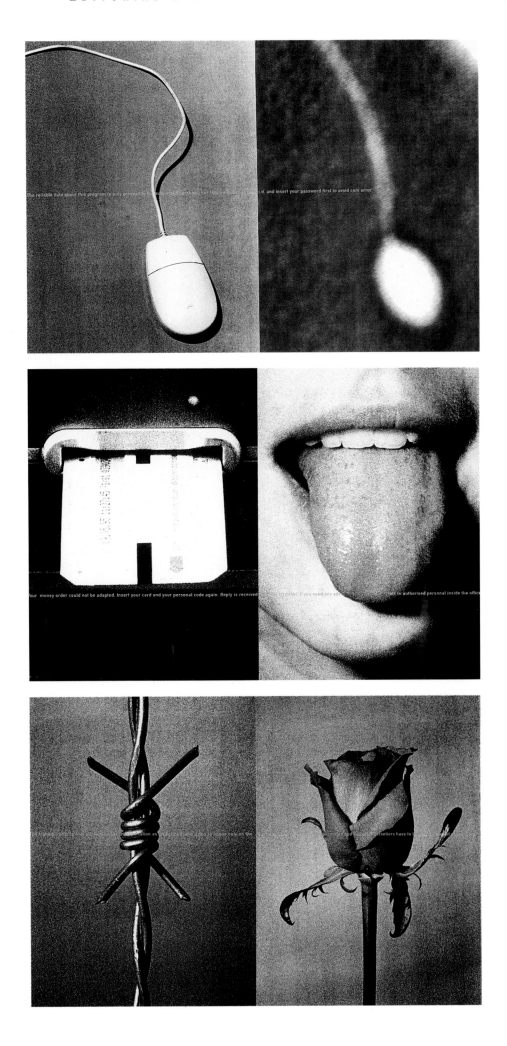

(THIS SPREAD)

STUDENT: GENES SOTTO

COLLEGE: CALIFORNIA COLLEGE OF ARTS & CRAFTS

DEGREE: BFA, GRAPHIC DESIGN

PROFESSOR: MICHAEL VANDERBYL

CLASS: GRAPHIC DESIGN FIVE

COUNTRY: USA

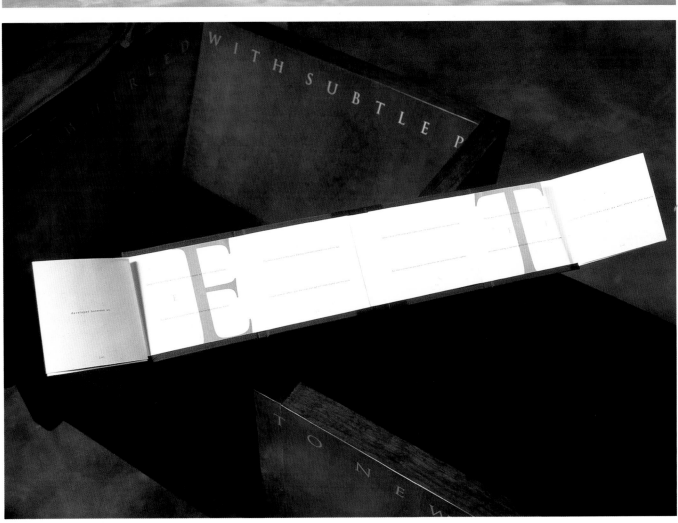

(THIS SPREAD)

STUDENT: CATHARINA SOESETYO

COLLEGE: CALIFORNIA COLLEGE OF ARTS & CRAFTS

DEGREE: BFA

PROFESSOR: MICHAEL VANDERBYL

CLASS: GRAPHIC DESIGN THESIS

COUNTRY: USA

■ 1 STUDENT: GIGI BIEDERMAN COLLEGE: CALIFORNIA COLLEGE OF ARTS & CRAFTS DEGREE: BFA IN GRAPHIC DESIGN PROFESSOR: MICHAEL VANDERBYL CLASS: GRAPHIC DESIGN THESIS COUNTRY: USA ■ 2, 3 STUDENT: SEOKHOON KIM COLLEGE: CALIFORNIA COLLEGE OF ARTS & CRAFTS DEGREE: BFA IN GRAPHIC DESIGN PROFESSOR: MICHAEL VANDERBYL CLASS: GRAPHIC DESIGN THESIS COUNTRY: USA

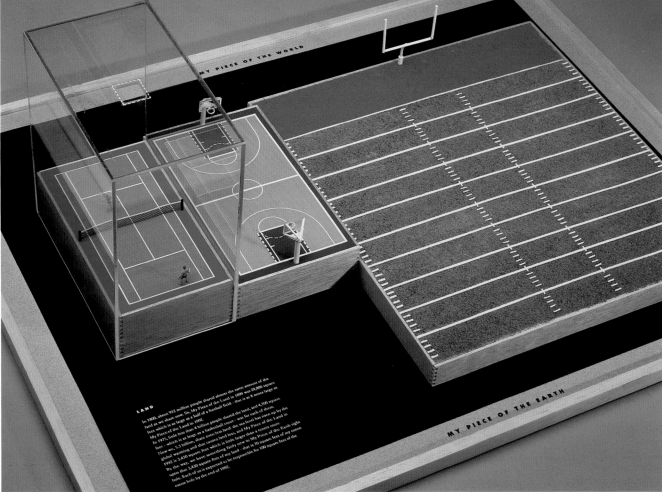

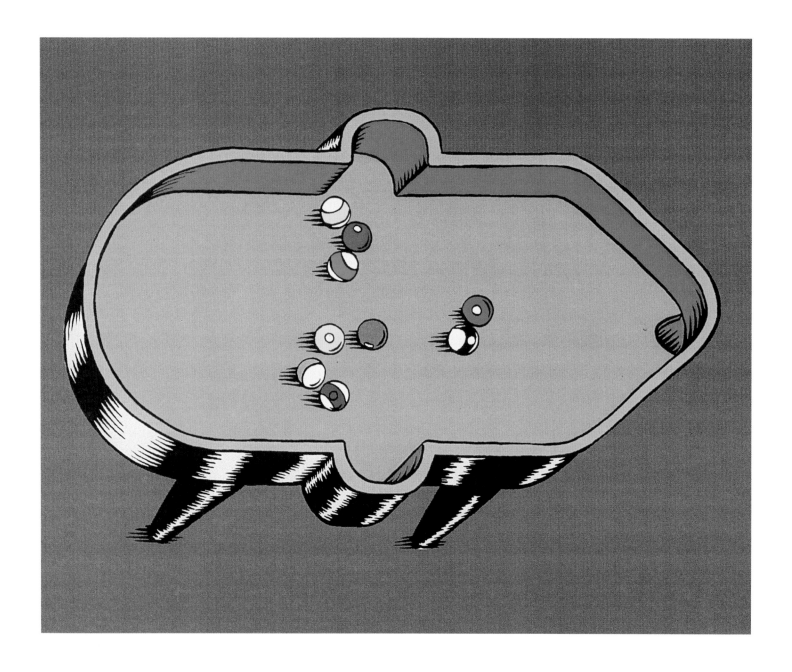

(THIS SPREAD)

STUDENT: CHRISTOPH NIEMANN

COLLEGE: STAATLICHE AKADEMIE DER BILDENDEN KÜNSTE STUTTGART

DEGREE: GRAPHIC DESIGN

PROFESSOR: HEINZ EDELMANN

CLASS: 4TH YEAR

COUNTRY: GERMANY

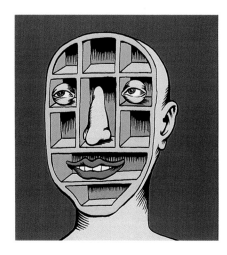
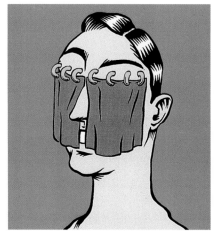
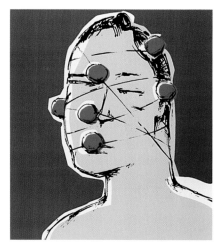
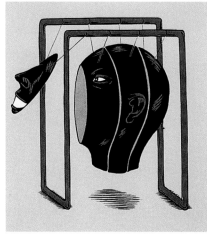

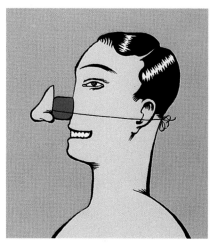
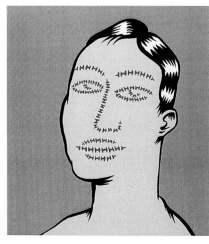
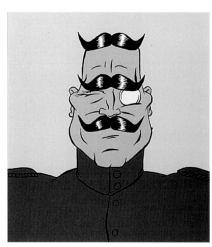

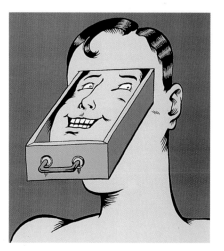

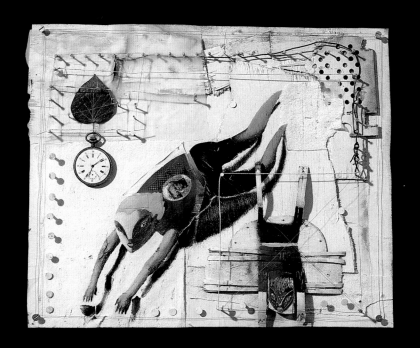

■ (PRECEDING SPREAD, ALL IMAGES) **1–3** Student: STEVEN TOSSIJN College: HOGESCHOOL SINT-LUKAS BRUSSEL Degree: GRAPHIC DESIGN Class: 4TH YEAR Country: BELGIUM ■ (THIS PAGE) **1–3** Student: PETER VASSIADIS College: VAKALO SCHOOL

OF ART AND DESIGN Degree: GRAPHIC DESIGN Professor: H. PANOPOULOS, D. PSOMAS Class: 2ND YEAR Country: GREECE ■ (OPPOSITE PAGE) **4** Student: KEITH TOWLER College: PORTFOLIO CENTER, GEORGIA Degree: ILLUSTRATION Country: USA

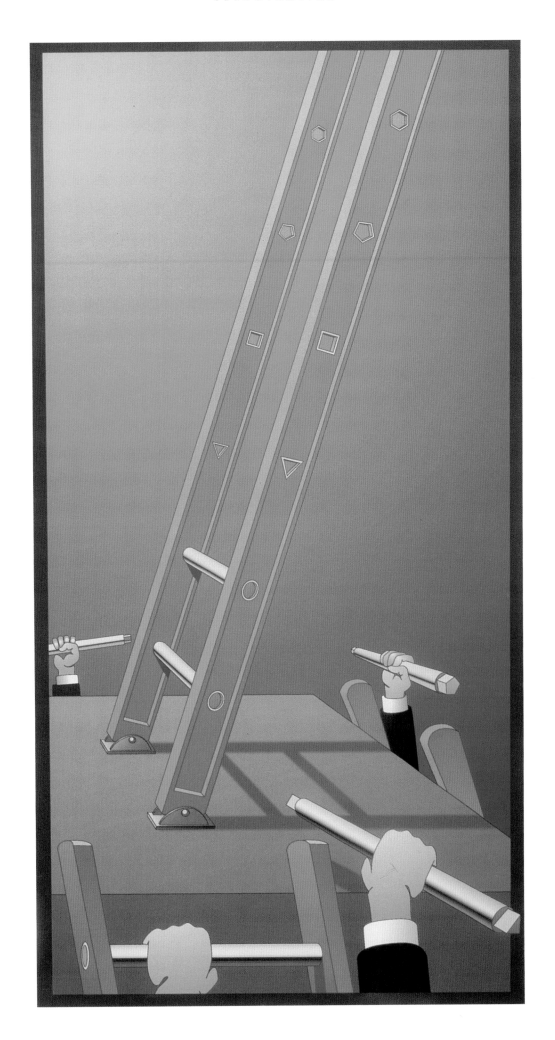

■ (ABOVE) **1** STUDENT: OLIVIER CALUWE COLLEGE: HOGESCHOOL SINT-LUKAS BRUSSEL DEGREE: MA GRAPHIC DESIGN CLASS: 4TH YEAR
COUNTRY: BELGIUM ■ (OPPOSITE PAGE) **2–4** STUDENT: XIAO ZHOU COLLEGE: RHODE ISLAND COLLEGE DEGREE: MA COUNTRY: USA

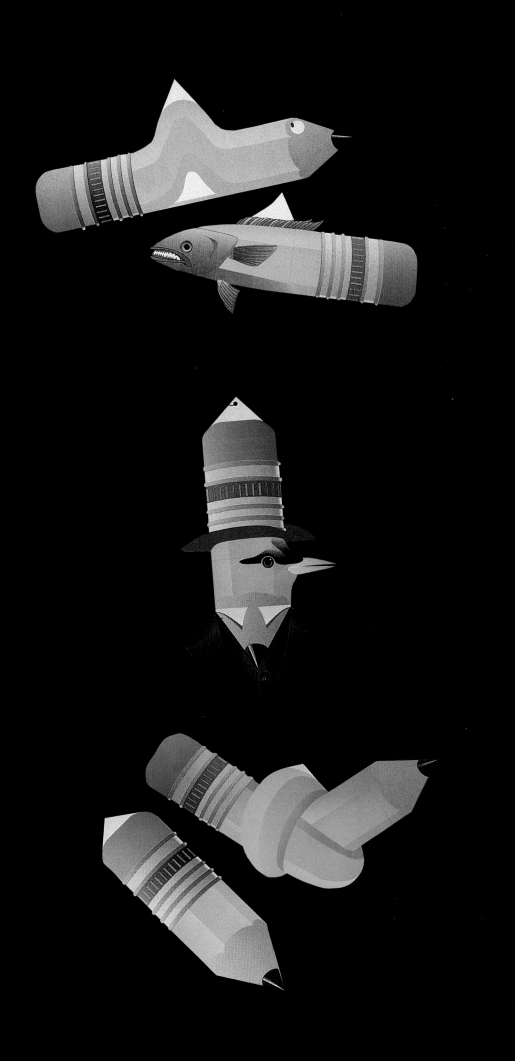

■ **1** STUDENT: BRUCE ERIKSON COLLEGE: EDINBORO UNIVERSITY OF PENNSYLVANIA DEGREE: BFA PROFESSOR: C.F. PAYNE COUNTRY: USA

■ **2** STUDENT: DONALD SIPLEY COLLEGE: SCHOOL OF VISUAL ARTS DEGREE: BFA COUNTRY: USA ■ **3** STUDENT: RE HAWKINS COLLEGE: O'MORE COLLEGE OF DESIGN DEGREE: GRAPHIC DESIGN PROFESSOR: BILL BARNES CLASS: PHOTOGRAPHY ART DIRECTION COUNTRY: USA

■ (OPPOSITE PAGE, TOP LEFT) **1** STUDENT: HIROYUKI SHIBATA COLLEGE: MT. VERNON NAZARENE COLLEGE DEGREE: BA COUNTRY: USA
■ (OPPOSITE TOP RIGHT) **2** STUDENT: AARON MESHON COLLEGE: RHODE ISLAND SCHOOL OF DESIGN DEGREE: BFA, ILLUSTRATION
PROFESSOR: ORA EITAN CLASS: "THE WRITTEN WORD" COUNTRY: USA ■ (OPPOSITE BOTTOM LEFT) **3** STUDENT: NANCY JAMES COLLEGE:
PORTFOLIO CENTER, GEORGIA DEGREE: ILLUSTRATION COUNTRY: USA ■ (OPPOSITE BOTTOM RIGHT) **4** STUDENT: DAVID EVANS
COLLEGE: VIRGINIA COMMONWEALTH UNIVERSITY DEGREE: BFA IN ILLUSTRATION PROFESSORS: ROBERT MEGANCK (EDITORIAL
ILLUSTRATION), ALEX BOSTIK (ILLUSTRATION IN BUSINESS COMMUNICATION) COUNTRY: USA ■ **5** (THIS PAGE) STUDENT: BOB ABRIC

COLLEGE: SACRED HEART UNIVERSITY PROFESSOR: JACK DE GRAFFENRIED CLASS: ILLUSTRATION I COUNTRY: USA ■ (FOLLOWING
SPREAD) **1–3** STUDENTS: GROUP PROJECT COLLEGE: INSTITUT SAINT-LUC DEGREE: GRAPHIC DESIGN PROFESSORS: JACQUELINE OST,
PAUL CROQUISON CLASS: COUNTRY: BELGIUM ■ **4, 6–9** STUDENT: THIMOTEUS WAGNER COLLEGE: UNIVERSITÄT ESSEN DEGREE: ADVER-
TISING PROFESSORS: VILLIM VASATA, OTTO NÄSCHER CLASS: 9TH TERM COUNTRY: GERMANY ■ **5** STUDENT: ARGIE MOUTAFIS COLLEGE:
SCHOOL OF VISUAL ARTS DEGREE: BFA PROFESSOR: ROBERT GOLDSTROM CLASS: SENIOR PORTFOLIO COUNTRY: USA ■ **10, 11** STUDENT:
PIERO CORVA COLLEGE: ISTITUTO EUROPEO DI DESIGN DEGREE: ILLUSTRATION CLASS: 4TH YEAR (GRADUATE CLASS) COUNTRY: ITALY

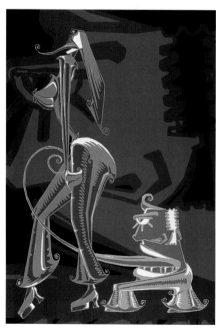
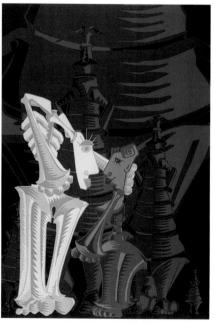
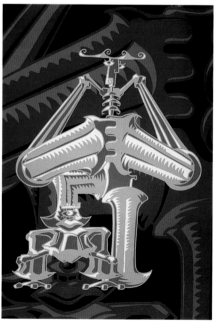

■ **1, 2** STUDENT: THOMAS FUCHS COLLEGE: KUNSTAKADEMIE STUTTGART DEGREE: GRAPHIC DESIGN PROFESSOR: HEINZ EDELMANN CLASS: 8TH TERM COUNTRY: GERMANY ■ **3** STUDENT: AARON MESHON COLLEGE: RHODE ISLAND SCHOOL OF DESIGN DEGREE: BFA IN ILLUSTRATION COUNTRY: USA ■ **4** STUDENT: MARIA-ELENA CONSTANTINESCU COLLEGE: ACADEMIE ROYALE DES BEAUX-ARTS DEGREE: ILLUSTRATION PROFESSOR: GILLES DEMOORTEL CLASS: GRADUATE CLASS COUNTRY: BELGIUM ■ **5** STUDENT: SUIT WONG

COLLEGE: SACRED HEART UNIVERSITY DEGREE: BFA PROFESSOR: JACK DE GRAFFENRIED COUNTRY: USA ■ **6** STUDENT: AARON D. VAUBEL COLLEGE: LINN-BENTON COMMUNITY COLLEGE DEGREE: AAS, GRAPHIC COMMUNICATIONS PROFESSOR: JOHN D. AIKMAN COUNTRY: USA ■ **7** STUDENT: BENJAMIN J. ZOLTEWICZ COLLEGE: CENTRAL CONNECTICUT STATE UNIVERSITY DEGREE: BA IN GRAPHIC DESIGN PROFESSORS: SUE VIAL, MARK STRATHY COUNTRY: USA ■ **8** STUDENT: STELLA PALLI COLLEGE: VAKALO SCHOOL OF ART AND DESIGN DEGREE: GRAPHIC DESIGN PROFESSOR: H. PANOPOULOS, D.PSOMAS CLASS: 2ND YEAR COUNTRY: GREECE

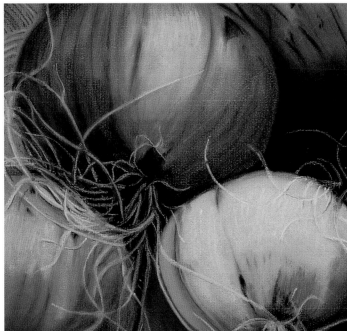

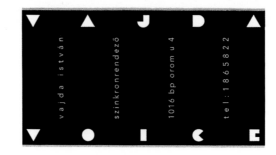

■ **1** Student: PÉTER VAJDA College: HUNGARIAN ACADEMY OF FINE ARTS Degree: GRAPHIC DESIGN Professors: GYÖRGY OLAH (GRAPHIC DESIGN), ATTILA AUTH (TYPOGRAPHY) Class: 2 NDYEAR Country: HUNGARY ■ **2** Student: GENES SOTTO College: CALIFORNIA COLLEGE OF ARTS & CRAFTS Degree: BFA IN GRAPHIC DESIGN Professor: JOHN BIELENBERG Class: TYPE 2 Country: USA

■ (FOLLOWING SPREAD, LEFT PAGE) **1** Student: JOYCE KOK College: OREGON STATE UNIVERSITY Degree: BFA IN GRAPHIC DESIGN Professor: DAVID HRADESTY Class: GRAPHIC DESIGN III Country: USA ■ (FOLLOWING SPREAD, RIGHT PAGE) **2, 3** Student: ANTHONY M. COOMBS College: KANSAS CITY ART INSTITUTE Degree: BFA Professor: SHARYN O'MARA Class: IMAGE II Country: USA

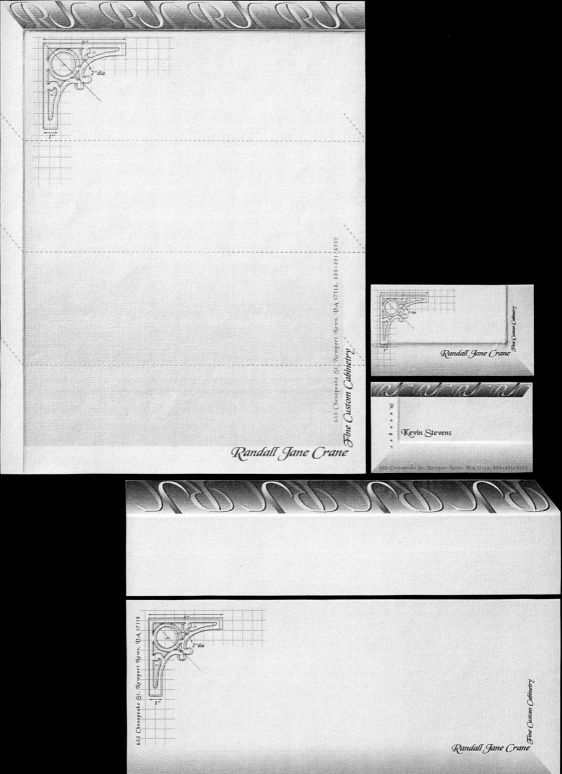

650 Chesapeake St. Newport News, VA 17118. 804-421-8252

Fine Custom Cabinetry

Randall Jane Crane

Fine Custom Cabinetry

Randall Jane Crane

Kevin Stevens

650 Chesapeake St. Newport News, VA 17118. 804-421-8252

650 Chesapeake St. Newport News, VA 17118

Fine Custom Cabinetry

Randall Jane Crane

epperson house
university of missouri-kansas city
5100 rockhill road
kansas city mo
64110-2499

ksu   ku   umkc

■ **1–7** STUDENT: HEINZ KUHN COLLEGE: FACHHOCHSCHULE KONSTANZ DEGREE: GRAPHIC DESIGN PROFESSOR: ANDERMATT CLASS: 4TH TERM

COUNTRY: GERMANY ■ **8** STUDENT: DAVE MCCLAIN COLLEGE: CALIFORNIA STATE UNIVERSITY, LONG BEACH DEGREE: BFA COUNTRY: USA

MOOSE McGILLYCUDDY'S
ANTLER ALE

©Dave McClain 1995

WHEELS
BIKE SHOP

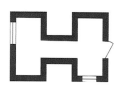

Logos

■ **1, 13** Student: Marshall Faircloth College: Portfolio Center, Georgia Degree: Graphic Design Country: USA ■ **2** Student: Daniel McQuillen College: Mercyhurst College Degree: Illustration Country: USA ■ **3** Students: Anna Suh, James A. Chilcutt, Jr., Dennis Brun, Natalie Mills Bontumasi College: University of Illinois, Chicago Degree: BFA Professors: John Greiner, John Massey Class: Team Project for the Chicago Cultural Center, International Congress, "Educating Cities, Arts & Humanities" Country: USA ■ **4, 7** Student: Michael K. Lum College: Portfolio Center, Georgia Degree: Graphic Design Professor: Mark Sandlin (4), Julie Sanders (7) Country: USA ■ **5, 11, 12** Student: Jonathan Selikoff College: Portfolio Center, Georgia Degree: Graphic Design Country: USA ■ **6** Student: Christoph Bolz College: Schule Für Gestaltung Bern Degree: Graphic Design Professor: Fritz Bürki Class: 3rd Year Country: Switzerland ■ **8** Student: Wendy Stamberger College: Kent State University Degree: BFA, Visual Communication Design Country: USA ■ **9** Student:

Shelley Antrobius College: Kent State University Degree: BFA, Graphic Design Professor: Bruce Morrill Class: Corporate ID Country: USA ■ **10** Student: Heinz Kuhn College: Fachhochschule Konstanz Degree: Communication Design Professor: Baviera Class: 4th Term Country: Germany ■ **14** Student: Hoai-Thuong Le College: Portfolio Center, Georgia Degree: Design Professor: Julie Sanders Class: Trademarks Country: USA ■ **15** Student: Jerry Lewis College: Portfolio Center, Georgia Degree: Design Country: USA ■ **16** Student: Ken Benedek College: Southwest Missouri State University Degree: BFA in Graphic Design Professor: Roman Duszek Class: Communication Design Country: USA ■ **17, 19** Student: William Jensen College: Mississippi State University Degree: Graphic Design Professor: Zoran Belic Class: Illustration I Country: USA ■ **18** Student: Augusta Duffy College: Portfolio Center, Georgia Degree: Design Country: USA ■ **20** Student: Thomas Riker College: Northern Arizona University Degree: Visual Communications Professor: Thomas Knights Country: USA

(THIS SPREAD)

STUDENT: GROUP PROJECT

COLLEGE: FACHHOCHSCHULE RHEINLAND-PFALZ, ABT. MAINZ 1

DEGREE: CORPORATE DESIGN

PROFESSOR: OLAF LEU

CLASS: GRADUATE

COUNTRY: GERMANY

CLASSIC TOYS

Classic Toys is an interactive collection that brings you back to your childhood. The user can travel back in time and explore different toys from the twenties to the present. The interactive control device guides the user through the nine decades of toys.

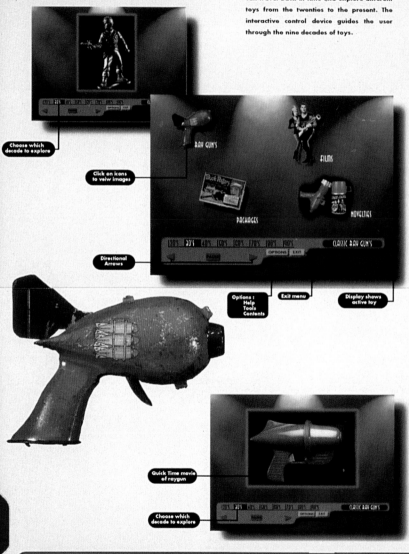

Choose which decade to explore

Click on icons to veiw images

Directional Arrows

Options :
Help
Tools
Contents

Exit menu

Display shows active toy

RAY GUN'S

FILMS

PACKAGES

NOVELTIES

Quick Time movie of raygun

Choose which decade to explore

The Processing of
Perception

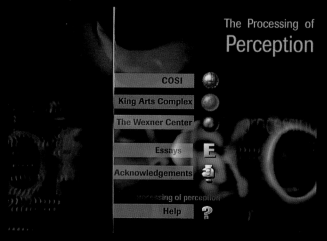

COSI

King Arts Complex

The Wexner Center

Essays   E

Acknowledgements

processing of perception

Help   ?

The Processing of
Perception

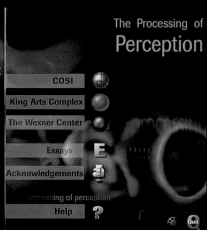

Our view of what is real is sometimes dependent on the view we have of that phenomenon. We have been told all our lives that we can trust in the truthfulness of something because we have a photograph of it. But recent examples have shown that modern imaging techniques allow a photograph to be modified in such a way that the change can't be detected — and therefore a processed perception of reality is presented as evidence to corroborate or verify the alleged matter of fact. Modern motion pictures are made without the restriction of a real set... technology has given us the ability to synthesize environments and even actors. And our view of worlds beyond the limits of our own has been expanded by virtue of imaging techniques applied to pictures beamed back to Earth from satellites passing even outside of our galaxy. It is this concept of technology that gives us the ability to process the data that comes to us in such a way that our perception of what is real is modified forever. This "Processing of Perception" is what is addressed in this exhibition. From interactive art to scientific visualizations, we are now able to view reality in a brand new way.

~Wayne Carlson

COSI

King Arts Complex

The Wexner Center

Essays   E

Acknowledgements

processing of perception

Help   ?   Quit

COSI

Richard Harned

John Huntington

Lorraine Justice

Midori Kitagawa De Leon

(Art)^n

Kiosks

COSI strives to provide an exciting and informative atmosphere for those of all ages to discover more about our environment, our accomplishments, our heritage, and ourselves. We hope to motivate a desire toward a better understanding of science, industry, health and history through involvement in exhibits, demonstrations, and a variety of activities and experiences. COSI is for the enrichment of the individual and for a more rewarding life on our planet, Earth.

King Arts Complex

Richard Harned

Nancy Patterson

Andrew F. Scott

InterFace

(Art)^n

Kiosks

Jennifer Liu   J

The Martin Luther King Jr. Performing and Cultural Arts Complex is committed to excellence in it's year round performing arts productions, visual arts exhibitions and culturally based educational activities. Through a multifaceted approach to exploring the African American experience the facility has forged a bridge of understanding between the people of Central Ohio and continues to stand at the cutting edge of service to both children and adults.

Seasons of Life 1994
Midori Kitagawa De Leon
Virtual 3D space on cibachrome prints

Computer animation is enabling artists, designers, and scientists to create new means of communication and exploration. Entertainers and advertisers produce non-existent worlds inhabited by imaginary creatures and impossible architecture. Computer visualization extends the perceptive powers of scientists and historians through time and space. Artists are given an ultimate tool of expression: the ability to control all aspects of a synthetic environment.

Kiosks

Blue Sky

The animation in the Kiosks has been provided by : Alpine View Images , A.K. Peters Ltd., Blue Sky Productions Inc., Yina Chang , Kevin Geiger , Peter Hriso , Lamb & Company, Inc. , Metrolight Studios , The Ohio Supercomputer Center , Pacific Data Images , Tonya Ramsey , S.E.A. , Inc. , Wen Hwa Seun , The University of North Carolina Department of Computer Science , The University of Minnesota Geometry Center , Windlight Studios , Xaos .

InterFace

Kevin Geiger and Wen Hwa Seun
InterFace 1995

John Huntington

John Huntington
Peter Hriso
Wen Hwa Seun
The Lomar Rail Visualization Project

1 STUDENT: GEORGE STAMOULIS COLLEGE: VAKALO SCHOOL OF ART AND DESIGN DEGREE: GRAPHIC DESIGN PROFESSORS: D. PSOMAS, S. SIMEONIDES CLASS: 3RD YEAR COUNTRY: GREECE ■ **2** STUDENT: DANAE KOUTSI COLLEGE: VAKALO SCHOOL OF ART AND DESIGN DEGREE: GRAPHIC

DESIGN PROFESSORS: H. PANOPOULOS, D. PSOMAS CLASS: 2ND YEAR COUNTRY: GREECE ■ **3** STUDENT: MATTHIAS BOIE COLLEGE: FACHHOCH-SCHULE RHEINLAND-PFALZ, ABT. MAINZ 1 DEGREE: CORPORATE IDENTITY DESIGN PROFESSOR: OLAF LEU CLASS: THESIS COUNTRY: GERMANY

(OPPOSITE PAGE) **1–3** STUDENT: LIANA ZAMORA COLLEGE: SCHOOL OF VISUAL ARTS DEGREE: BACHELOR OF FINE ARTS PROFESSOR: MARY ANN SALVATO JONES COUNTRY: USA ■ (THIS PAGE) **4** STUDENT: AKIKO AMANO COLLEGE: CALIFORNIA STATE UNIVERSITY LOS ANGELES DEGREE: B.A, DESIGN PROFESSOR: MICHAEL HENDERSON CLASS: GRAPHIC DESIGN I COUNTRY: USA

■ (THIS PAGE) **1** STUDENT: NILS MARTENS COLLEGE: FACHHOCHSCHULE AUGSBURG DEGREE: COMMUNICATIONS CLASS: 9TH TERM PROFESSORS: HEITMANN, FUNK COUNTRY: GERMANY ■ (OPPOSITE TOP AND BOTTOM) **2, 4** STUDENT: TOM KIRSCH COLLEGE: EAST TEXAS STATE UNIVERITY

DEGREE: B.S. IN DESIGN COMMUNICATIONS PROFESSOR: DAVID BECK CLASS: DESIGN III COUNTRY: USA ■ (OPPOSITE CENTER) **3** STUDENT: MATT WOOLMAN COLLEGE: VIRGINIA COMMONWEALTH UNIVERSITY DEGREE: MFA IN DESIGN/VISUAL COMMUNICATIONS COUNTRY: USA

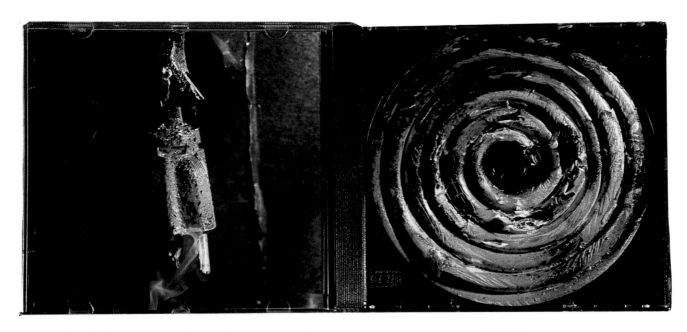

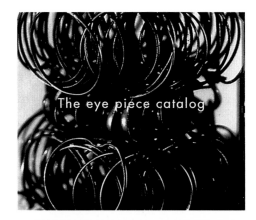

THE HISTORY OF THE EYE PIECE IS A BIT FUZZY, BUT IT SEEMS THAT EYEGLASSES WERE MOST LIKELY INVENTED SIMULTANEOUSLY during the 13th century in Italy and china. Because few people could read or owned books, and because glasses were so expensive, wearing them was a symbol of wisdom and wealth. Some 14th-century aristocrats wore them without lenses simply to appear more intelligent. The earliest lenses were made of glass or transparent stones, and since they were convex, they were only useful to farsighted people, to help with reading and close vision. Concave lenes, for nearsighted people, were not invented until the early 15th century. It was not until the mid-17th century that eyeglasses with rigid temples were introduced which meant they finally stopped sliding off the nose.

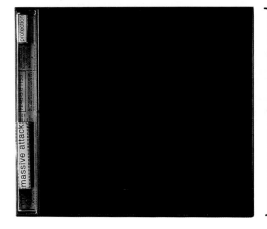

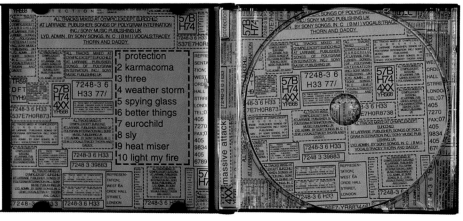

■ 1, 2 STUDENT: DANIEL AMADE COLLEGE: RINGLING SCHOOL OF ART & DESIGN DEGREE: BFA PROFESSOR: KIMBERLY ELAM CLASS: GRAPHIC DESIGN STUDIO COUNTRY: USA ■ 3 STUDENT: MILER HUNG COLLEGE: TEXAS CHRISTIAN UNIVERSITY PROFESSOR: LEWIS GLAZER CLASS: COMPUTER GRAPHIC COUNTRY: USA ■ 4 STUDENT: HOLLY AQUILAR COLLEGE: TEXAS CHRISTIAN UNIVERSITY DEGREE:

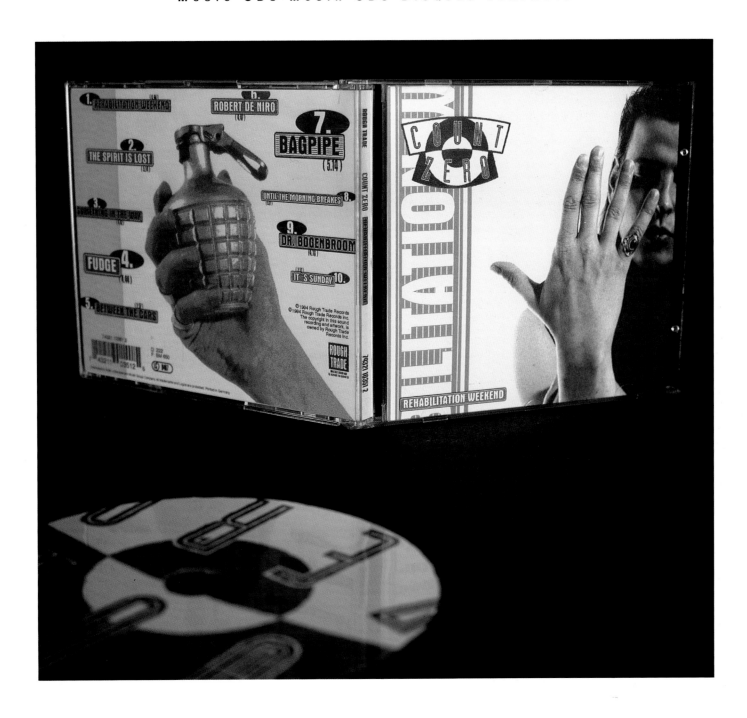

COMMUNICATION GRAPHICS PROFESSOR: LEWIS GLASER COUNTRY: USA ■5, 6 STUDENT: DAVID BYUN COLLEGE: SCHOOL OF VISUAL ARTS DEGREE: BFA IN GRAPHIC DESIGN PROFESSOR: CHIP KIDD COUNTRY: USA ■7 STUDENT: JENS DOMMERMUTH COLLEGE: FACHHOCHSCHULE DORTMUND DEGREE: GRAPHIC DESIGN PROFESSORS: DIETER HILBIG, DIETER ZIEGENFEUTER CLASS: 6TH YEAR COUNTRY: GERMANY

■ 1 STUDENT: ELIZABETH BENATOR COLLEGE: PORTFOLIO CENTER, GEORGIA DEGREE: DESIGN COUNTRY: USA ■ 2, 3 STUDENT: MILER HUNG COLLEGE: TEXAS CHRISTIAN UNIVERSITY PROFESSORS: MARGIE ADKINS, ALAN LIDJI, LEWIS GLAZER COUNTRY: USA ■ 4, 5 STUDENT: NATHAN PULVER COLLEGE: BOWLING GREEN STATE UNIVERSITY DEGREE: GRAPHIC DESIGN PROFESSOR: SHERWOOD MCBROOM CLASS: PACKAGING COUNTRY: USA

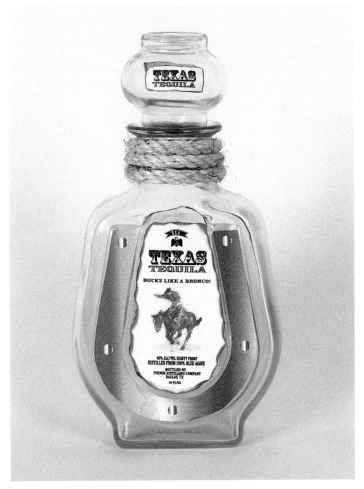

■ 1 STUDENT: JOHN SMALLMAN COLLEGE: WESTERN WASHINGTON UNIVERSITY DEGREE: BA IN STUDIO ARTS, GRAPHIC DESIGN CONCENTRATION PROFESSOR: KENT SMITH COUNTRY: USA ■ 2 STUDENT: GRETCHEN LEARY COLLEGE: PENN STATE UNIVERSITY DEGREE: BA IN GRAPHIC DESIGN PROFESSOR: KRISTIN BRESLIN SOMMESE COUNTRY: USA ■ 3 STUDENT: PATRICIA MENDELSOHN COLLEGE: GEORGIA STATE UNIVERSITY DEGREE: BFA IN GRAPHIC DESIGN PROFESSOR: CHARLES ATKINS CLASS: TYPOGRAPHY COUNTRY: USA ■ 4 STUDENT: AMY

ANSTINE COLLEGE: PENN STATE UNIVERSITY DEGREE: BA IN GRAPHIC DESIGN PROFESSOR: KRISTIN BRESLIN SOMMESE CLASS: PACKAGING COUNTRY: USA ■ 5 STUDENT: PAULA M. BICKFORD COLLEGE: GEORGIA STATE UNIVERSITY DEGREE: BFA IN GRAPHIC DESIGN COUNTRY: USA ■ 6 STUDENT: SOOK LIM COLLEGE: GEORGIA STATE UNIVERSITY DEGREE: BFA PROFESSOR: CHARLES AKINS CLASS: CORPORATE IDENTITY COUNTRY: USA ■ 7 STUDENT: MARGARET CAIN COLLEGE: PORTFOLIO CENTER, GEORGIA DEGREE: PHOTOGRAPHY COUNTRY: USA

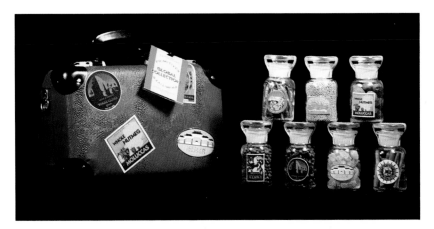

■ **1** Student: MATTHIAS BOIE College: FACHHOCHSCHULE RHEINLAND-PFALZ, ABT. MAINZ 1 Degree: CORPORATE D'ESIGN Professor: OLAF LEU Class: THESIS Country: GERMANY ■ **2** Student: GLADYS YUE College: PARSONS SCHOOL OF DESIGN Degree: BFA Professor: KERRI KONIK Class: JUNIOR PACKAGING Country: USA ■ **3** Student: GREG DICKERSON College: EDINBORO UNIVERSITY OF PENNSYLVANIA Degree: BFA IN APPLIED MEDIA, GRAPHIC DESIGN Professor: DIANE CRANDAL Country: USA ■ **4** Student: CLAUDIA KRUG College: BLOCHERER SCHULE Degree: GRAPHIC DESIGN Professor: KLAUS MÜLLER Class: 8TH TERM Country: GERMANY

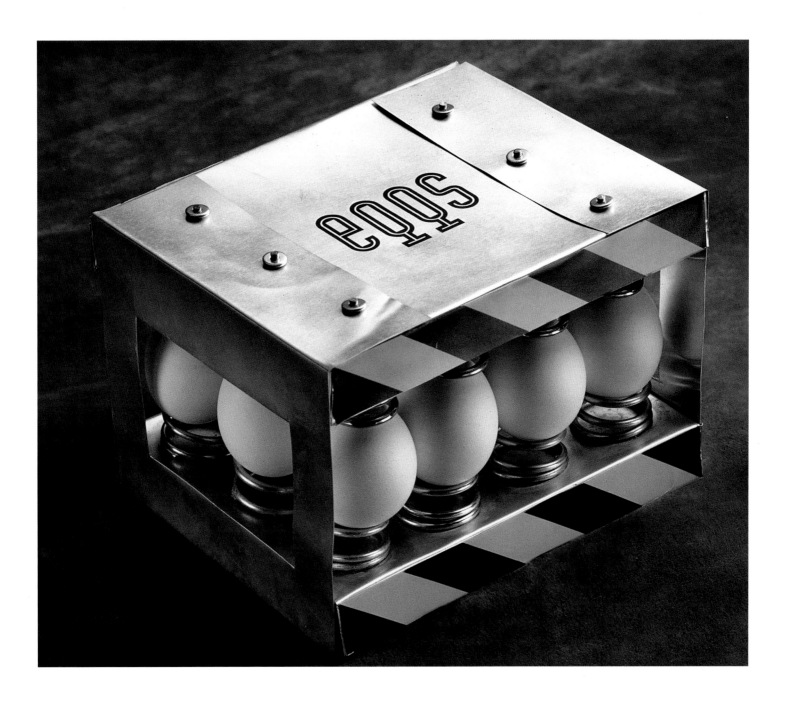

■ (OPPOSITE PAGE) **1** Student: JASON COHEN College: PENN STATE UNIVERSITY Degree: BA IN GRAPHIC DESIGN
Professor: KRISTIN BRESLIN SOMMESE Class: PACKAGING Country: USA ■ (THIS PAGE) **2** Student: BRIAN HARRISON
College: EAST TEXAS STATE UNIVERSITY Degree: COMMUNICATION ARTS DESIGN Professor: DAVID BECK Country: USA

161

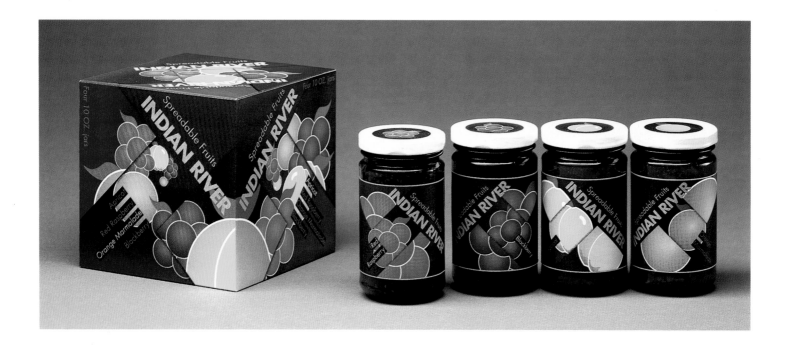

■ (THIS PAGE AND OPPOSITE TOP) **1, 2** STUDENT: PADRAIG C. MCCOBB COLLEGE: OREGON STATE UNIVERSITY DEGREE: BFA IN GRAPHIC DESIGN PROFESSOR: DAVID P. HARDESTY CLASS: GRAPHIC DESIGN III COUNTRY: USA ■ **3** (OPPOSITE BOTTOM) STUDENT: MARI ANN TALBOT COLLEGE: KUTZTOWN UNIVERSITY DEGREE: BFA IN COMMUNICATION DESIGN CLASS: PACKAGE DESIGN COUNTRY: USA

■ (THIS PAGE) **1** STUDENT: LIZ WHITAKER COLLEGE: PENN STATE UNIVERSITY DEGREE: BACHELOR IN GRAPHIC DESIGN PROFESSOR: KRISTIN BRESLIN SOMMESE COUNTRY: USA ■ (OPPOSITE PAGE TOP) **2** STUDENT: GROUP PROJECT COLLEGE: FACHHOCH-

SCHULE RHEINLAND-PFALZ, ABT. MAINZ **1** DEGREE: CORPORATE IDENTITY DESIGN PROFESSOR: OLAF LEU COUNTRY: GERMANY ■ (OPPOSITE PAGE BOTTOM) **3** STUDENT: ALEX MCKEITHAN COLLEGE: PORTFOLIO CENTER, GEORGIA DEGREE: DESIGN COUNTRY: USA

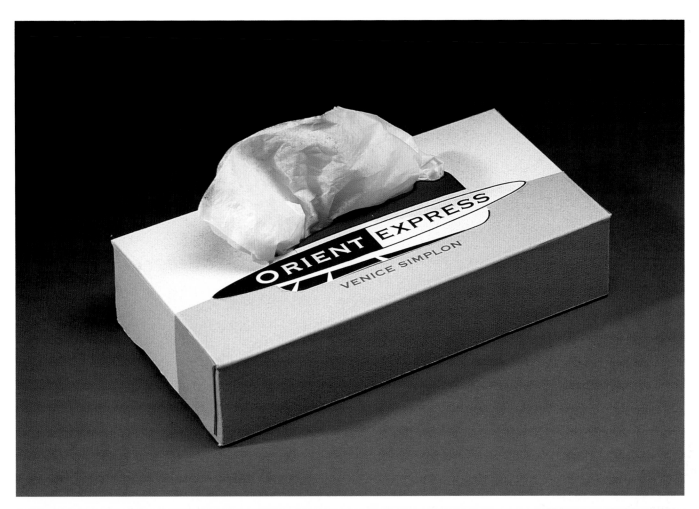

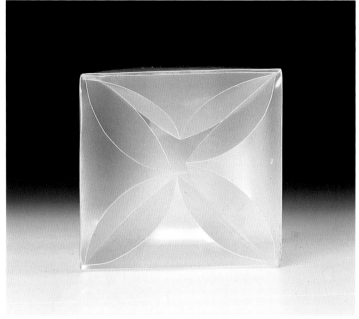

■ **1, 2** STUDENT: LESLEY ZINN COLLEGE: PURCHASE COLLEGE, S.U.N.Y. DEGREE: BFA PROJECT SPONSOR: PHIL ZIMMERMAN COUNTRY: USA ■

3 STUDENT: HEIDI LENZ COLLEGE: SAN DIEGO CITY COLLEGE DEGREE: BFA, GRAPHIC DESIGN PROFESSOR: CANDACE LOPEZ COUNTRY: USA

■ 1, 2 Student: LESLEY ZINN College: PURCHASE COLLEGE, S.U.N.Y. Degree: BFA Project Sponsor: PHIL ZIMMERMAN Class: SENIOR PROJECT Country: USA ■ 3, 4 Student: CHIN-LIEN CHEN College: RHODE ISLAND SCHOOL OF DESIGN Degree: BFA Professor: AKI NUROSI Class: PACKAGE DESIGN Country: USA ■ 5 Student: CHRIS TSERNJAVSKI College: SWINBURNE SCHOOL OF DESIGN Degree: BACHELOR OF GRAPHIC DESIGN Lecturers: HELMUT LUECKENHAUSEN, JOHN BASSANI Country: AUSTRALIA

■ **1** STUDENT: TOM KIRSCH COLLEGE: EAST TEXAS STATE UNIVERSITY DEGREE: BS, DESIGN COMMUNICATIONS PROFESSOR: CERITA SMITH CLASS: BASIC TYPOGRAPHY COUNTRY: USA ■ **2** STUDENT: ALEXANDER HELDT COLLEGE: HOCHSCHULE FÜR KÜNSTE BREMEN

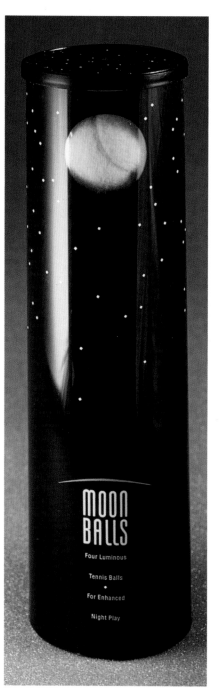

PROFESSOR: WOLFGANG JARCHOV COUNTRY: GERMANY ■ **3, 4** STUDENT: NATALIE RENARD COLLEGE: PENN STATE UNIVERSITY DEGREE: BACHELOR OF GRAPHIC DESIGN PROFESSOR: KRISTIN BRESLIN SOMMESE CLASS: PACKAGING DESIGN COUNTRY: USA

■ (THIS PAGE) **1–6** STUDENT: YESMIN CHAN COLLEGE: UNIVERSITY OF NORTHUMBIA DEGREE: MA, GRAPHIC DESIGN COUNTRY: GREAT BRITAIN ■ (OPPOSITE PAGE) **7** STUDENT: MANFRED KOH COLLEGE: PORTFOLIO CENTER, GEORGIA DEGREE: PHOTOGRAPHY COUNTRY: USA

(THIS SPREAD)

STUDENT: RICHARD UNGER

COLLEGE: UNIVERSITÄT/GH ESSEN

DEGREE: PHOTODESIGN

PROFESSOR: ERICH VOM ENDT

CLASS: 10TH TERM

COUNTRY: GERMANY

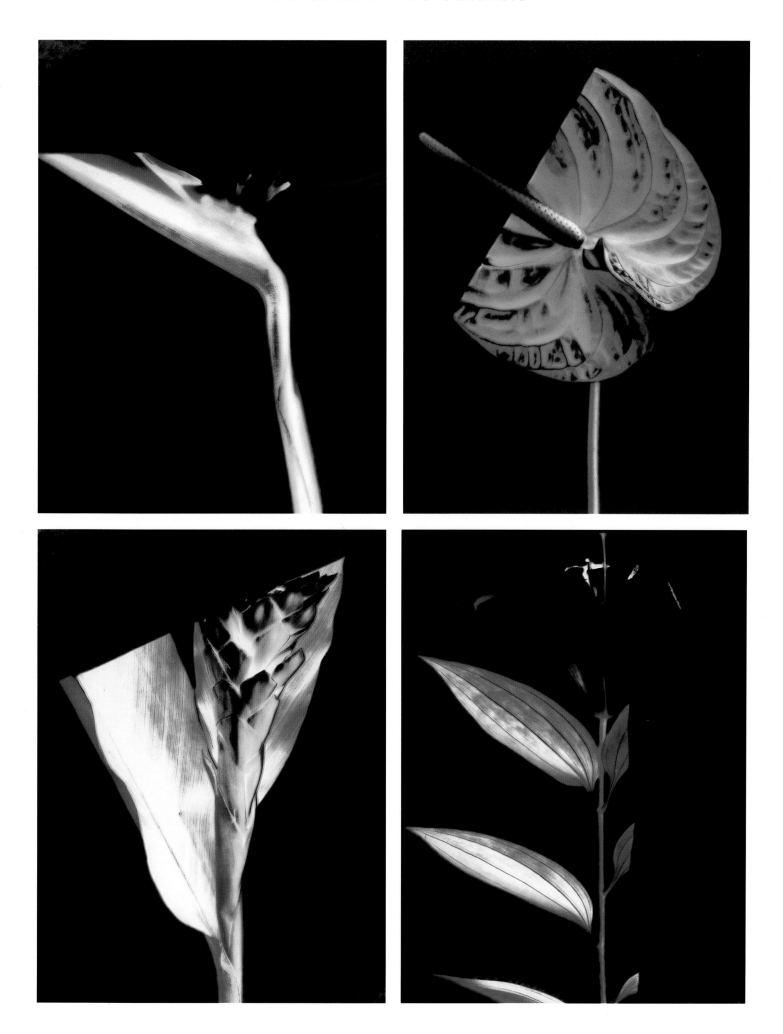

■ (THIS PAGE TOP) **1** Student: CLAUDIA LOPEZ College: PORTFOLIO CENTER, GEORGIA Degree: PHOTOGRAPHY Country: USA

■ (THIS PAGE BOTTOM) **2** Student: MARGARET CAIN College: PORTFOLIO CENTER, GEORGIA Degree: PHOTOGRAPHY Country: USA

(THIS PAGE) **3** STUDENT: HORACE HICKS COLLEGE: PORTFOLIO CENTER, GEORGIA DEGREE: PHOTOGRAPHY COUNTRY: USA

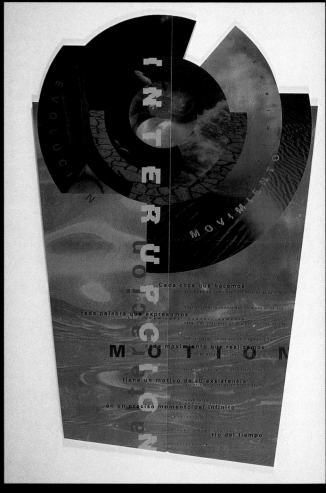

■ 1 STUDENT: BEATE INGRID ACKERMANN COLLEGE: MARYLAND INSTITUTE, COLLEGE OF ART DEGREE: BFA IN VISUAL COMMUNICATION/
DESIGN PROFESSOR: ELIZABETH NEAD COUNTRY: USA ■ 2 STUDENT: SIOJAN YAGUI COLLEGE: RINGLING SCHOOL OF ART AND DESIGN
PROFESSOR: POLLY JOHNSON CLASS: GRAPHIC DESIGN STUDIO COUNTRY: USA ■ 3 STUDENT: LEIGH MUELLER COLLEGE: TEXAS CHRISTIAN
UNIVERSITY DEGREE: COMMUNICATION GRAPHICS PROFESSOR: LEWIS GLASER CLASS: COMMUNICATION GRAPHICS II COUNTRY: USA

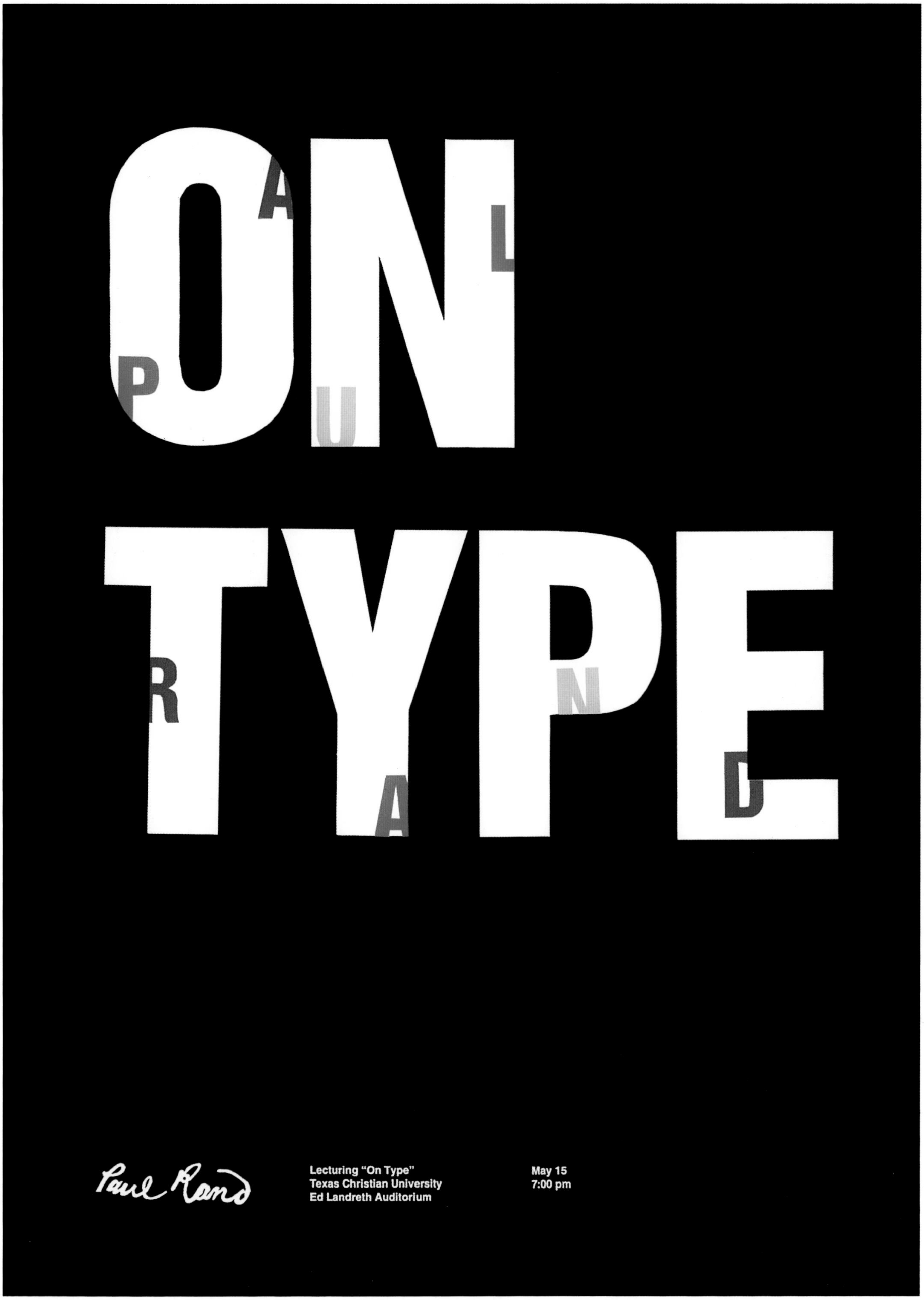

ON TYPE

PAUL RAND

Paul Rand

Lecturing "On Type"
Texas Christian University
Ed Landreth Auditorium

May 15
7:00 pm

■ 1, 2 Student: FRANK SCHAWERNA College: UNIVERSITÄT ESSEN Degree: COMMUNICATION DESIGN Professors: VOLKER KÜSTER, PAUL SCHÜLLNER, VILLIM VASATA, INGE OSSWALD Class: 8TH TERM Country: GERMANY ■ 3 Student: GLORIA G. GALANG College: UNIVERSITY

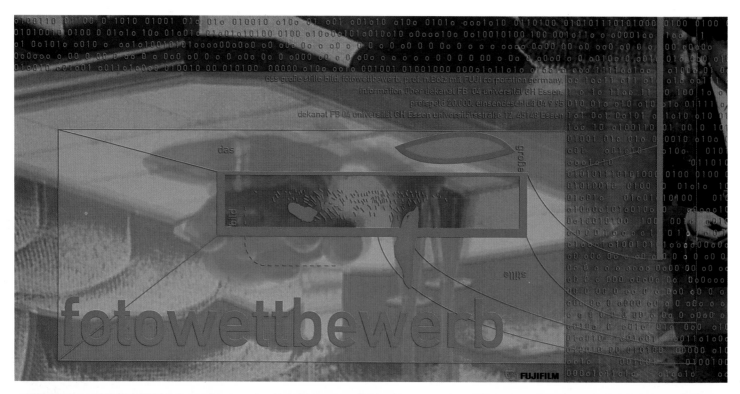

OF CALIFORNIA AT SANTA BARBARA Degree: BA IN ART STUDIO Professor: VICTORIA VESNA Class: ART STUDIO 22/122 Country: USA ■
4 Student: NICHOLAS GREENING College: THE SWINBURNE SCHOOL OF DESIGN Degree: BACHELOR OF DESIGN Country: AUSTRALIA

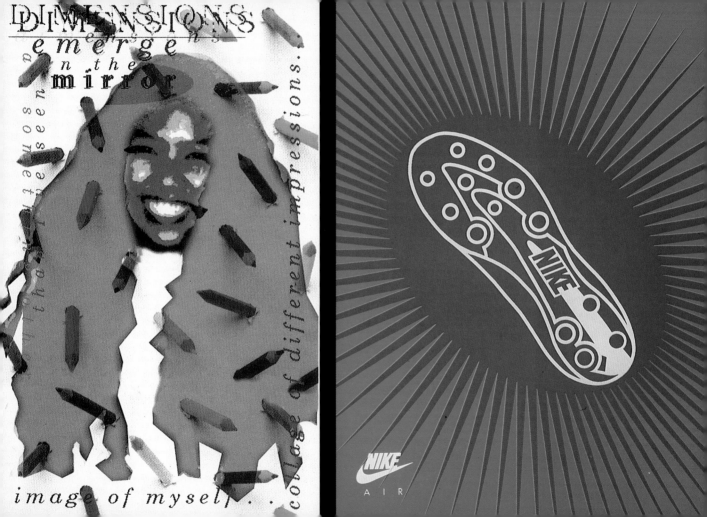

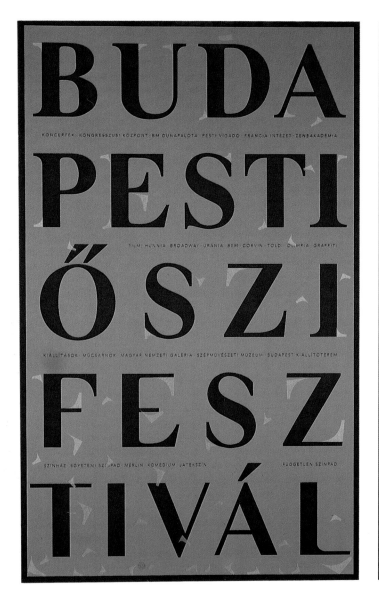

■ (THIS PAGE) 1, 2 STUDENT: PÉTER VAJDA COLLEGE: HUNGARIAN ACADEMY OF FINE ARTS PROFESSORS: GYÖRGY OLAH (GRAPHIC DESIGN), ATTILA AUTH (TYPOGRAPHY) CLASS: 2ND YEAR COUNTRY: HUNGARY ■ (OPPOSITE PAGE) 3 STUDENT: DAVID TREWERN COLLEGE: THE SWINBURNE SCHOOL OF DESIGN DEGREE: BACHELOR OF DESIGN LECTURER: JOHN BASSANI COUNTRY: AUSTRALIA

International
Architecture
Convention

World Congress Centre Melbourne. August 20 to 23, 1994. Hosted by The Royal Australian Institute of Architects.

Keynote Speakers: Santiago Calatrava, Daniel Libeskind, Michael Sorkin, Harry Seidler, John Denton.

Planning

Evolution

1994

■ 1 Student: JEFFREY JAY MOORE College: CALIFORNIA STATE UNIVERSITY, LONG BEACH Degree: VISUAL COMMUNICATION/GRAPHIC DESIGN Professor: JIM VAN EIMEREN Country: USA ■ 2 Student: ERIC HOLLER College: RINGLING SCHOOL OF ART AND DESIGN Degree: BFA Professor: POLLY JOHNSON Class: GRAPHIC DESIGN STUDIO Country: USA ■ 3 Student: PATRICIA EVANGELISTA College:

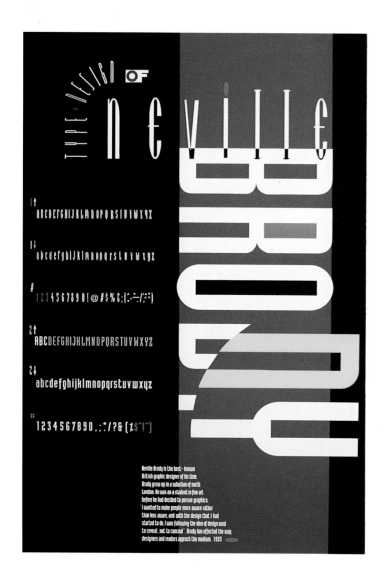

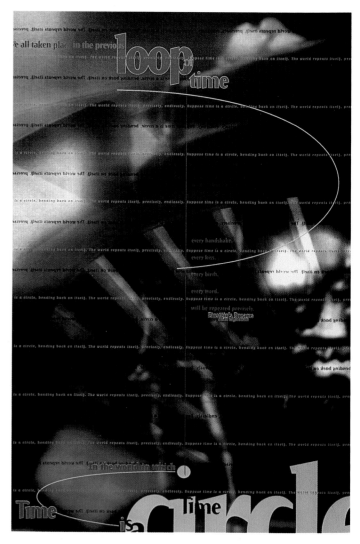

CALIFORNIA COLLEGE OF ARTS AND CRAFTS Degree: GRAPHIC DESIGN Professor: DOUG AKAGI Class: GRAPHIC DESIGN I Country: USA ■ 4 Student: GELINA AVGERINOU College: VAKALO SCHOOL OF ART AND DESIGN Degree: GRAPHIC DESIGN Professor: H. HARALAMBOUS Class: 3RD YEAR Country: GREECE ■ 5 Student: HAMID RAHMANIAN Designer: FARHAD FARSI College: PRATT INSTITUTE Country: USA ■ 6 Student: LOURDES T. BAÑEZ College: SCHOOL OF VISUAL ARTS Degree: BFA IN GRAPHIC DESIGN Country: USA

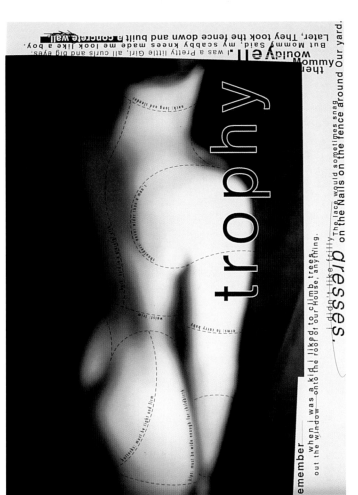

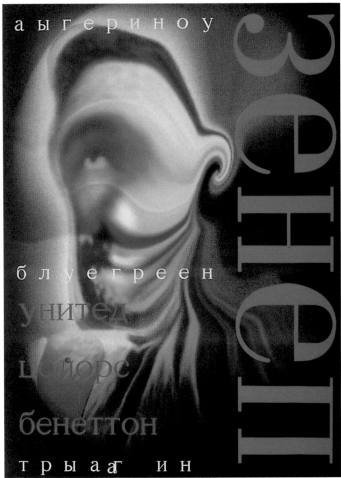

Mark Sandman is in the kitchen of his Cambridge loft, squishing up tuna, mayonnaise and relish with a fork. "Anybody want a sandwich?" he asks no one in particular, then begins judiciously chopping some celery. He smiles wryly, his persona reminiscent of the character John Lurie played in Stranger Than Paradise. "This is my cocoon," he continues, waving his hand around the loft. "I never leave, especially when it's cold outside. My friends come by and bring me sandwiches and cigarettes."

Sandman is the bass player, singer and lyrical soul of Morphine, a band whose music seems somewhat cocoon-like as well. The group's 1992...

Morphine

ON THE ROAD >

MaIDS

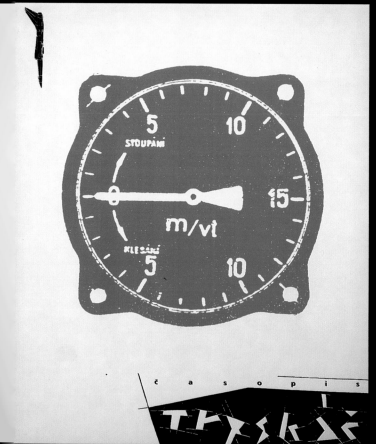

5   10

STOUPÁNÍ

15

m/vt

KLESÁNÍ

5   10

č a s o p i s

FREE YOUR BEER

Heineken®

■ 1 STUDENT: PO LING LAI COLLEGE: SAVANNAH COLLEGE OF ART AND DESIGN DEGREE: BFA PROFESSOR: FATHI BAKKOUSH CLASS: ALTERNATIVE DESIGN APPROACH COUNTRY: USA ■ 2 STUDENT: YOOMI CHONG COLLEGE: SCHOOL OF VISUAL ARTS DEGREE: BFA COUNTRY: USA ■ 3 STUDENT: PETER BABÁK COLLEGE: ACADEMY OF ARTS, ARCHITECTURE AND DESIGN PRAGUE PROFESSOR: JAN SOLPERA CLASS: STUDIO OF BOOK GRAPHICS AND LETTERING COUNTRY: CZECH REPUBLIC ■ 4 STUDENT: ELENA KACHRILAS COLLEGE:

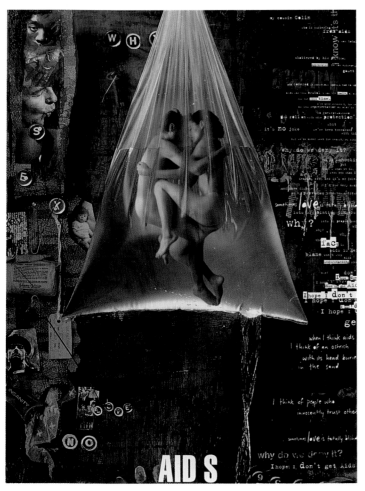

VAKALO SCHOOL OF ART AND DESIGN DEGREE: GRAPHIC DESIGN PROFESSORS: PSOMAS, SIMEONIDES, KANAKAKI CLASS: 3RD YEAR COUNTRY: GREECE ■ 5 STUDENTS: TODD MITCHELL, ADAM FOX, GARTH DAVIS, CHRIS TSERNJAVSKI COLLEGE: THE SWINBURNE SCHOOL OF DESIGN DEGREE: BACHELOR OF DESIGN LECTURERS: HELMUT LUECKENHAUSEN, JOHN BASSAM COUNTRY: AUSTRALIA ■ 6 STUDENT: ANNABEL DUNDAS COLLEGE: THE SWINBURNE SCHOOL OF DESIGN DEGREE: BACHELOR OF DESIGN COUNTRY: AUSTRALIA

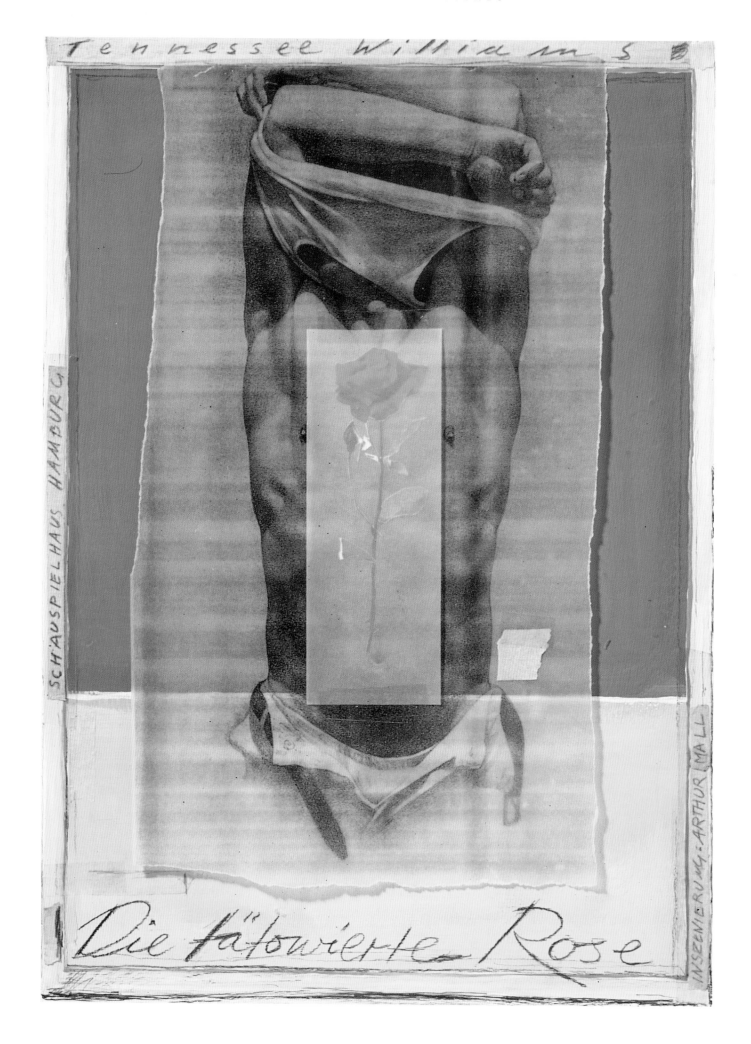

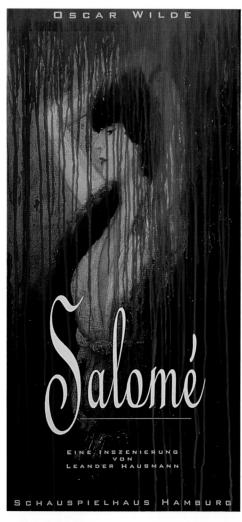

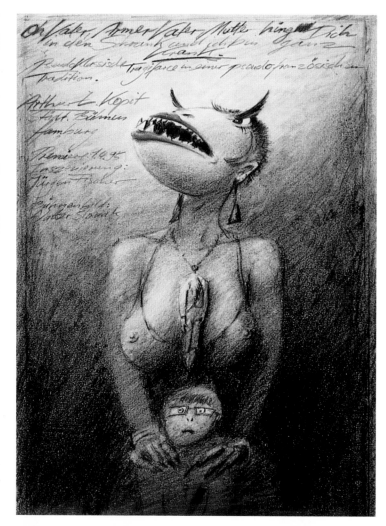

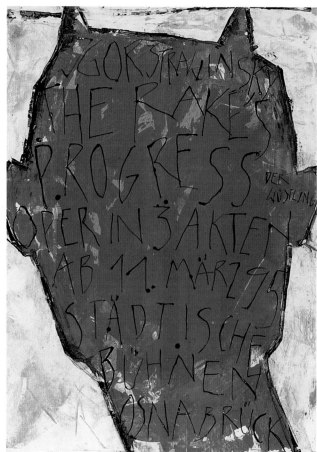

(PRECEDING SPREAD LEFT) **1** STUDENT: HANS HEINRICH SURES COLLEGE: FACHHOCHSCHULE DORTMUND, FACHBEREICH DESIGN DEGREE: GRAPHIC DESIGN PROFESSOR: ZIEGENFEUTER CLASS: 10TH TERM COUNTRY: GERMANY ■ (PRECEDING SPREAD RIGHT) **2** STUDENT: EVA NOTHOMB COLLEGE: INSTITUT SAINT-LUC DEGREE: GRAPHIC DESIGN PROFESSOR: SOPHIE BERTOT CLASS: GRADUATE CLASS COUNTRY: BELGIUM ■ (OPPOSITE TOP) **1, 2** STUDENT: HANS HEINRICH SURES COLLEGE: FACHHOCHSCHULE DORTMUND, FACHBEREICH DESIGN DEGREE: GRAPHIC DESIGN PROFESSOR: ZIEGENFEUTER CLASS: 10TH TERM COUNTRY: GERMANY ■ **3** (OPPOSITE

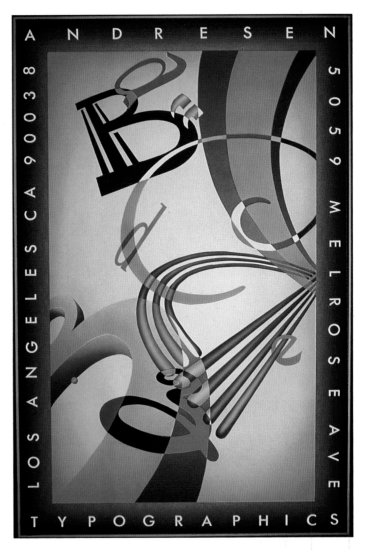

BOTTOM LEFT) STUDENT: YOOMI CHONG COLLEGE: SCHOOL OF VISUAL ARTS DEGREE: BFA COUNTRY: USA ■ (OPPOSITE BOTTOM RIGHT) **4** STUDENT: NINA PAGALIES COLLEGE: HOCHSCHULE FÜR KÜNSTE BREMEN DEGREE: GRAPHIC DESIGN PROFESSOR: BERND BEXTE COUNTRY: GERMANY ■ (ABOVE LEFT) **5** STUDENT: GARRETT MATSUDAIRA COLLEGE: WESTERN WASHINGTON UNIVERSITY DEGREE: BACHELOR OF ARTS PROFESSOR: KENT SMITH CLASS: ADVANCED TYPOGRAPHY COUNTRY: USA ■ (RIGHT) **6** STUDENT: JEFFREY JAY MOORE COLLEGE: CALIFORNIA STATE UNIVERSITY, LONG BEACH DEGREE: VISUAL COMMUNICATION/GRAPHIC DESIGN PROFESSOR: TOM HALL COUNTRY: USA

(THIS PAGE) **1** Student: SONJA KAMPCZYK (WINNER OF THE FIRST PRIZE OF THE COMPETITION "PROMETHEUS AND HIS CREATURES: THE ARTIFICIAL MAN FROM THE ANCIENT WORLD TO THE PRESENT DAY") College: BERGISCHE UNIVERSITÄT WUPPERTAL Degree: COMMUNICATION DESIGN Professor: UWE LOESCH Country: GERMANY ■ (OPPOSITE TOP) **2** Student: MARK FROWEIN (FINALIST, 7TH INTERNATIONAL DESIGN COMPETITION OSAKA 1995) College: BERGISCHE UNIVERSITÄT WUPPERTAL Degree: COMMUNICATION

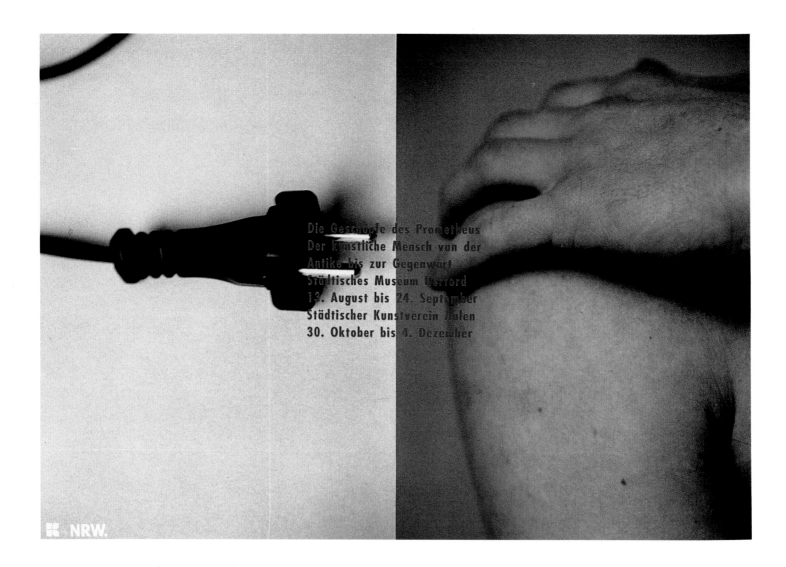

DESIGN Professor: UWE LOESCH Country: GERMANY ■ **3** Student: OLIVER VAUPEL (WINNER OF THE FIRST PRIZE IN THE COMPETITION "SECOND CONGRESS OF FURTHER EDUCTION, NRW 1994") College: BERGISCHE UNIVERSITÄT WUPPERTAL Degree: COMMUNICATION DESIGN Professor: UWE LOESCH Country: GERMANY ■ (CENTER) **4** Student: BEN BUSCHFELD College: BERGISCHE UNIVERSITÄT WUPPERTAL Degree: COMMUNICATION DESIGN Professor: UWE LOESCH Country: GERMANY ■ (BOTTOM) **5** Student: JAN FEDERMANN College: BERGISCHE UNIVERSITÄT WUPPERTAL Degree: COMMUNICATION DESIGN Professor: UWE LOESCH Country: GERMANY

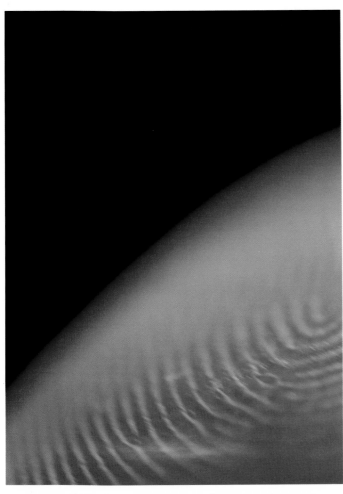

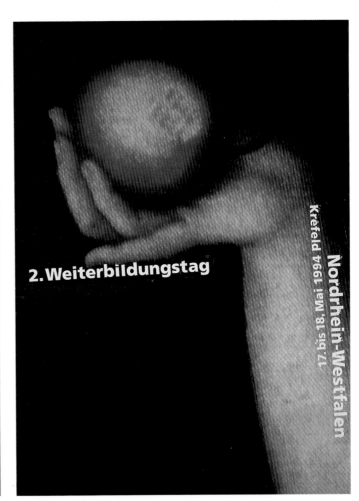

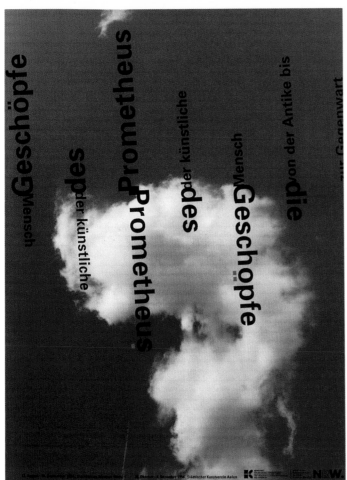

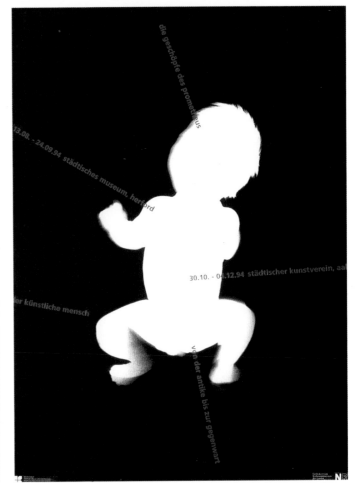

■ **1** STUDENT: DAVE SIMON COLLEGE: CALIFORNIA COLLEGE OF ARTS AND CRAFTS DEGREE: INDUSTRIAL DESIGN PROFESSOR: MARTIN LINDER CHAIRMAN: STEVEN SKOV HOLT CLASS: PRODUCT DESIGN I COUNTRY: USA ■ **2** STUDENT: MARTIN ZECH COLLEGE: HOCHSCHULE FÜR KÜNSTE BREMEN DEGREE: GRAPHIC DESIGN (DIPLOM-GRAPHIK-DESIGNER) PROFESSOR: GÜNTHER WEHMANN COUNTRY: GERMANY ■

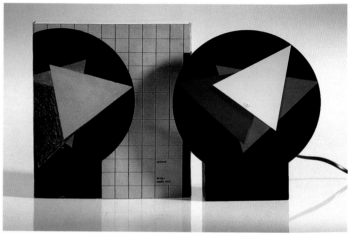

3, 4 STUDENT: JO ROPER COLLEGE: COLCHESTER INSTITUTE DEGREE: BA HONS PROFESSOR: DAVID JURY CLASS: 3RD YEAR COUNTRY: GREAT BRITAIN ■ **5, 6** STUDENT: CAROLINE FLAGIELLO COLLEGE: CALIFORNIA COLLEGE OF ARTS AND CRAFTS DEGREE: BFA IN PRODUCT DESIGN PROFESSOR: STEVEN SKOV HOLT COUNTRY: USA ■ **7, 8** STUDENT: JONAH BECKER COLLEGE: CALIFORNIA COLLEGE OF ARTS AND CRAFTS DEGREE: INDUSTRIAL DESIGN PROFESSOR: STEVEN SKOV HOLT CLASS: INDUSTRIAL DESIGN I COUNTRY: USA

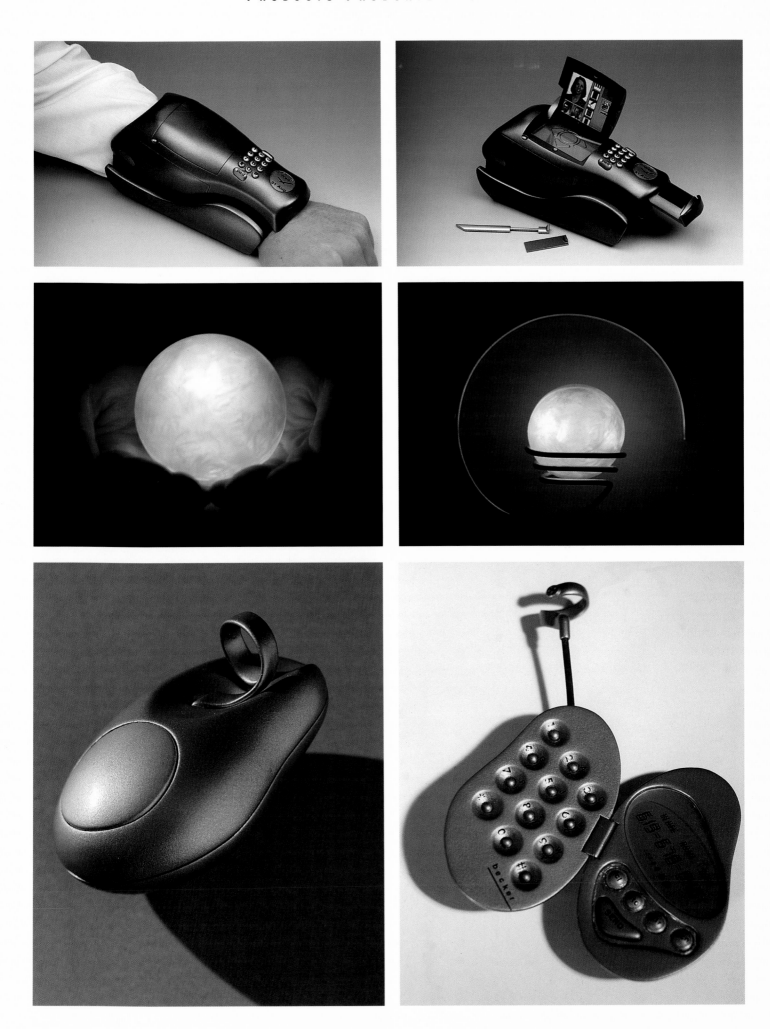

■ (THIS PAGE LEFT AND OPPOSITE BOTTOM) **1, 4** Student: WILL WEAR College: CALIFORNIA COLLEGE OF ARTS AND CRAFTS Degree: INDUSTRIAL DESIGN Professor: WHITNEY SANDER Chairman: STEVEN SKOV HOLT Class: INDUSTRIAL DESIGN II Country: USA ■ (THIS

PAGE RIGHT AND OPPOSITE TOP) **2, 3** Student: CORY COVINGTON College: CALIFORNIA COLLEGE OF ARTS AND CRAFTS Degree: INDUSTRIAL DESIGN Professor: MARTIN LINDER Chairman: STEVEN SKOV HOLT Class: DESIGN OF FURNITURE FOR INDUSTRY Country: USA

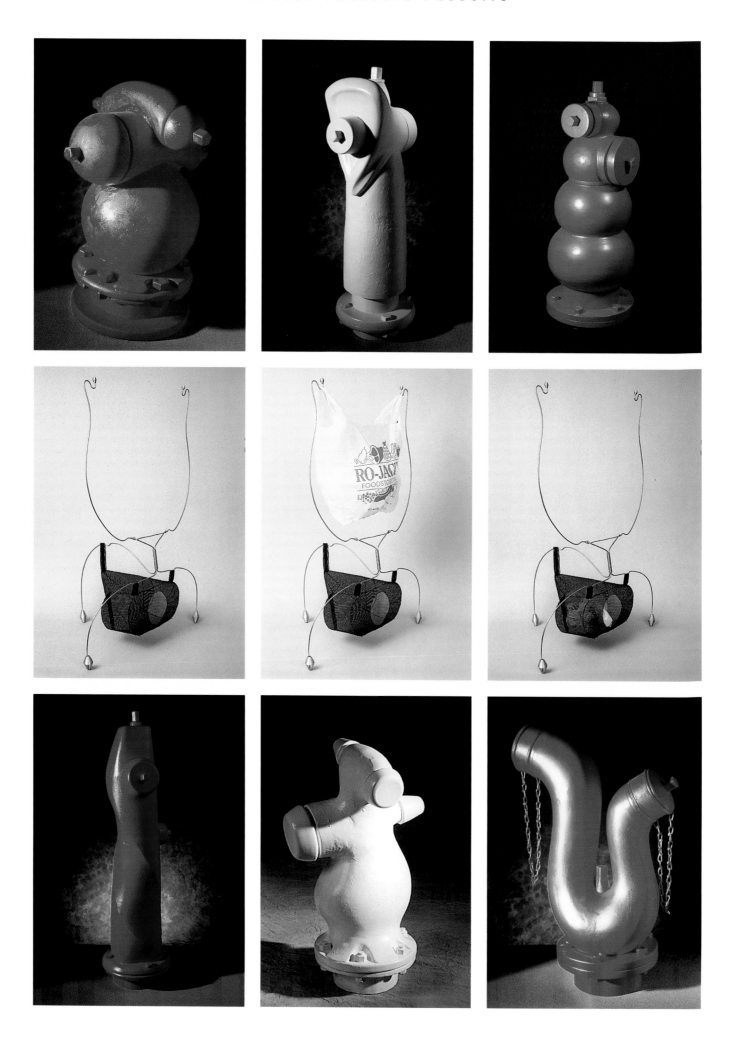

■ 1 Student: JENNIFER RAPUANO College: CALIFORNIA COLLEGE OF ARTS AND CRAFTS Degree: BFA IN INDUSTRIAL DESIGN Professor: STEVE PEART Chairman: STEVEN SKOV HOLT Class: INDUSTRIAL DESIGN IV Country: USA ■ 2 Student: DOMINIQUE HATT College: CALIFORNIA COLLEGE OF ARTS AND CRAFTS Degree: BFA IN INDUSTRIAL DESIGN Professor: STEVE PEART Chairman: STEVEN SKOV HOLT Country: USA ■ 3 Student: CORY COVINGTON College: CALIFORNIA COLLEGE OF ARTS AND CRAFTS Degree: INDUSTRIAL DESIGN Professor: STEPHEN PEART Chairman: STEVEN SKOV HOLT Class: INDUSTRIAL DESIGN IV Country: USA ■ 4–6 Student: JAMES PITTMAN College: PRATT INSTITUTE Degree: MASTERS IN INDUSTRIAL DESIGN Professor: LEN BACICH, REBECCA

WELZ Country: USA ■ 7 Student: SANDRA HESLA College: CALIFORNIA COLLEGE OF ARTS AND CRAFTS Degree: BFA IN INDUSTRIAL DESIGN Professor: STEVE PEART Chairman: STEVEN SKOV HOLT Class: INDUSTRIAL DESIGN IV Country: USA ■ 8 Student: BENSON LAM College: CALIFORNIA COLLEGE OF ARTS AND CRAFTS Degree: BFA IN INDUSTRIAL DESIGN Chairman: STEVEN SKOV HOLT Country: USA ■ 9 Student: DEBRA MARTIN College: CALIFORNIA COLLEGE OF ARTS AND CRAFTS Degree: BFA IN INDUSTRIAL DESIGN Professor: STEPHEN PEART Chairman: STEVEN SKOV HOLT Class: INDUSTRIAL DESIGN IV Country: USA ■ 10 Students: RICHARD UNGER, CHRISTOPH SCHUHKNECHT College: UNIVERSITÄT/GH ESSEN, FACHBEREICH 4 Class: 10TH TERM Country: GERMANY

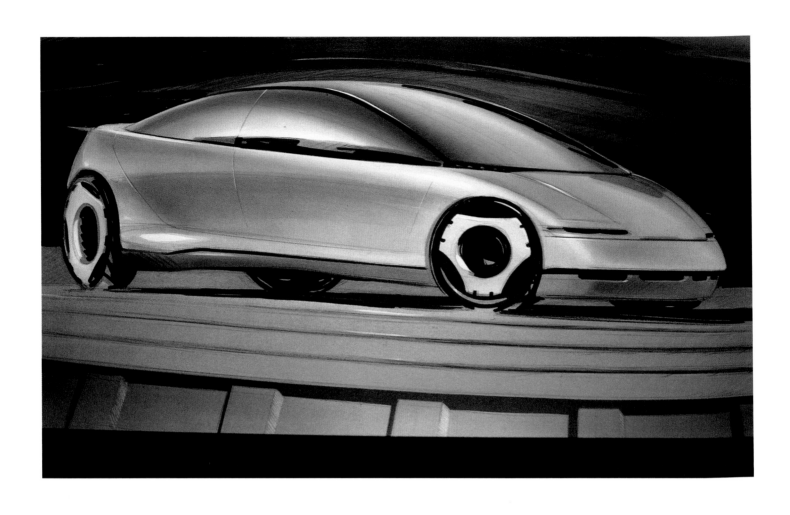

■ **1** (THIS PAGE) Student: TOURAJ TONI BAYAT College: CALIFORNIA STATE UNIVERSITY, LONG BEACH Degree: B.S., INDUSTRIAL DESIGN Country: USA ■ (OPPOSITE PAGE ALL IMAGES) **2–6** Student: ANNA H. SUH College: UNIVERSITY OF ILLINOIS, CHICAGO Degree: BFA, GRAPHIC DESIGN Professor: JOHN GREINER Class: GRAPHIC DESIGN VI Country: USA

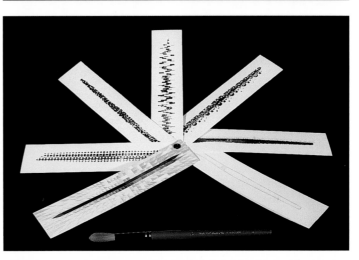

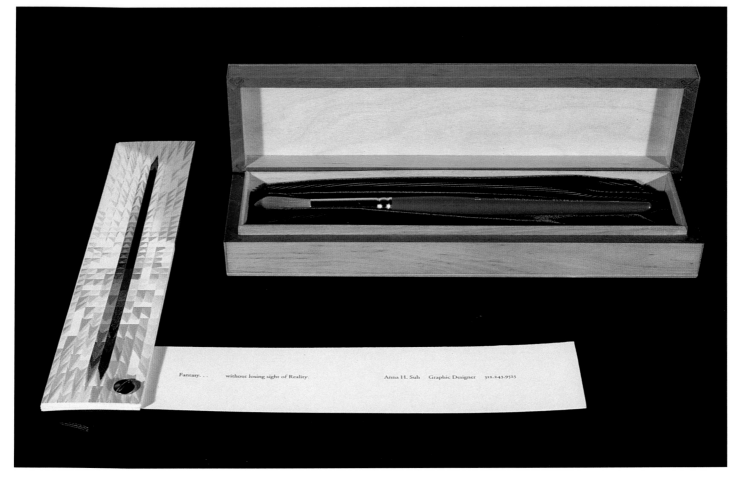

1. DU MÅ IKKE HAVE ANDRE
GUDER END MIG

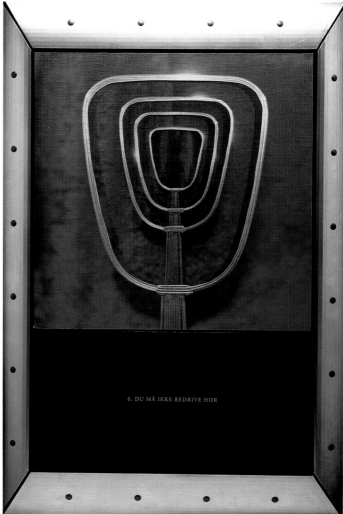

6. DU MÅ IKKE BEDRIVE HOR

(THIS SPREAD)
STUDENT: LISBETH EUGENIE CHRISTENSEN
COLLEGE: THE COLLEGE OF ARTS, CRAFTS AND DESIGN KOLDING
DEGREE: GRAPHIC DESIGN
CLASS: 5TH YEAR (GRADUATE CLASS)
COUNTRY: DENMARK

5. DU MÅ IKKE SLÅ IHJEL

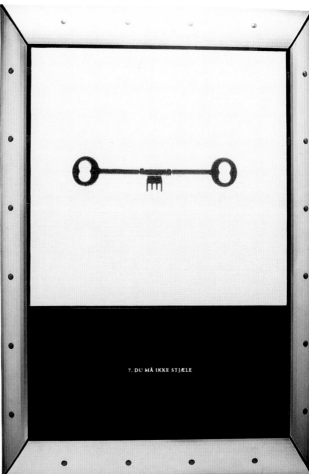

7. DU MÅ IKKE STJÆLE

8. DU MÅ IKKE SIGE FALSK VIDNESBYRD
MOD DIN NÆSTE

10. DU MÅ IKKE BEGÆRE DIN NÆSTES HUSTRU, HANS
TRÆL ELLER TRÆLKVINDE, HANS OKSE ELLER ÆSEL
ELLER NOGET, DER HØRER DIN NÆSTE TIL

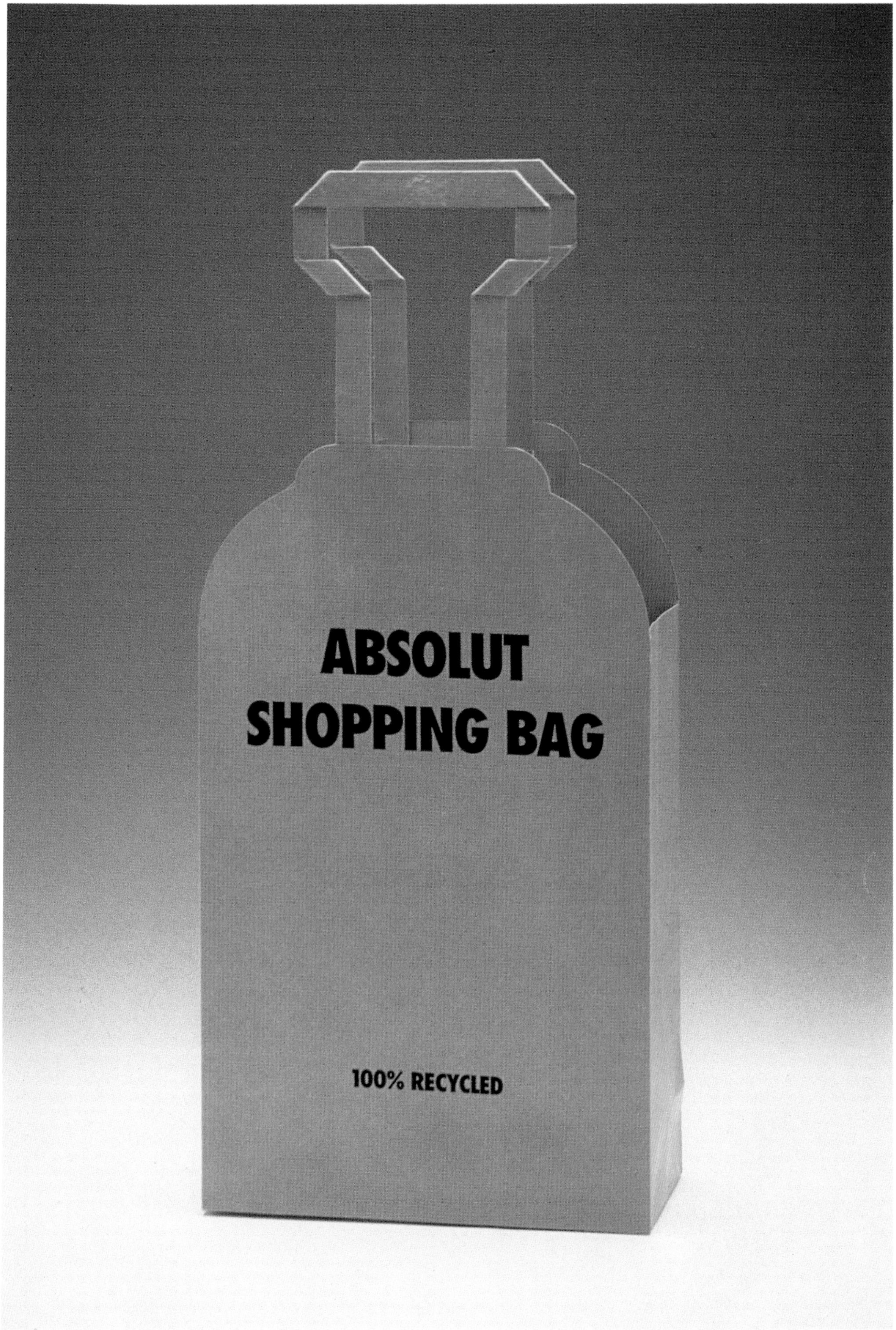
ABSOLUT
SHOPPING BAG
100% RECYCLED

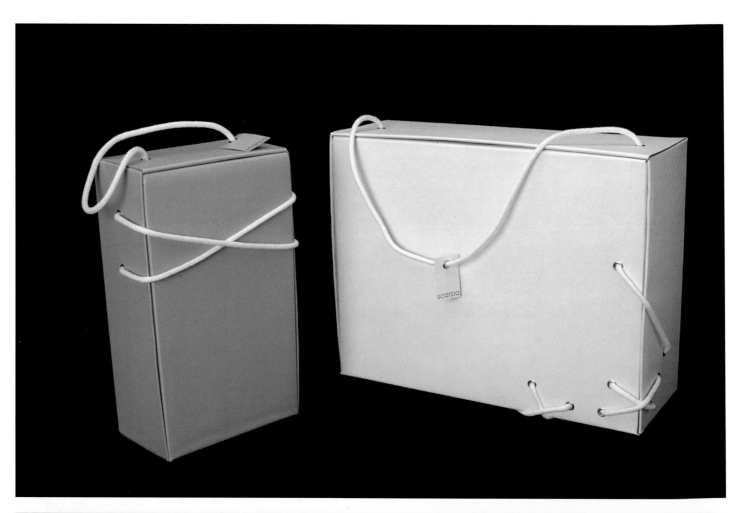

■ (PRECEDING SPREAD LEFT) **1** STUDENT: CHRISTIAN WERNER COLLEGE: PENN STATE UNIVERSITY DEGREE: BA IN GRAPHIC DESIGN PROFESSOR: KRISTIN BRESLIN SOMMESE CLASS: PACKAGING COUNTRY: USA ■ (PRECEDING SPREAD RIGHT) **2** STUDENT: FRIDOLIN T. BEISERT COLLEGE: ART CENTER (EUROPE) COUNTRY: SWITZERLAND ■ (OPPOSITE PAGE TOP) **1** STUDENT: BRIDGETTE KLOECKER

COLLEGE: PENN STATE UNIVERSITY DEGREE: BA IN GRAPHIC DESIGN PROFESSOR: KRISTIN BRESLIN SOMMESE CLASS: PACKAGING COUNTRY: USA ■ (OPPOSITE PAGE BOTTOM) **2** STUDENT: ELLEN KYUNG KIM COLLEGE: PENN STATE UNIVERSITY DEGREE: BA IN GRAPHIC DESIGN PROFESSOR: LANNY SOMMESE, KRISTIN BRESLIN SOMMESE COUNTRY: USA ■ (THIS PAGE) **3** STUDENT: JENN MILLER COLLEGE: PENN STATE UNIVERSITY DEGREE: BA IN GRAPHIC DESIGN PROFESSOR: KRISTIN BRESLIN SOMMESE COUNTRY: USA

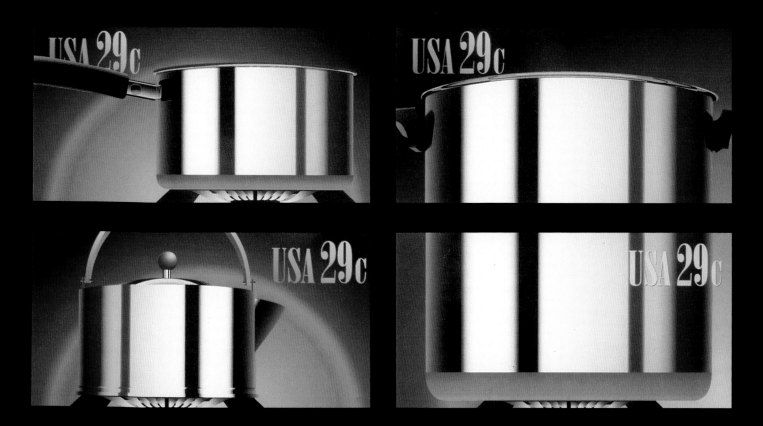

■ **1** STUDENT: BARBARA C. COFFEY COLLEGE: AMERICAN ACADEMY OF ART DEGREE: ASSOCIATE OF APPLIED SCIENCE IN COMMERCIAL ART PROFESSOR: DOROTHY MCSHERRY CLASS: GRAPHIC DESIGN 202 COUNTRY: USA ■ (OPPOSITE TOP) **2** STUDENT: KEITH TOWLER COLLEGE: PORTFOLIO CENTER, GEORGIA DEGREE: ILLUSTRATION COUNTRY: USA ■ (OPPOSITE BOTTOM) **3** STUDENT: YOSHIHISA OSHIMA COLLEGE: RHODE ISLAND SCHOOL OF DESIGN DEGREE: BA IN GRAPHIC DESIGN PROFESSOR: KRZYSZTOF LENK CLASS: DEGREE PROJECT COUNTRY: USA

ABCDEFG
abcdefghi
HIJKLMN!
jklmnopqr
OPQRST?
1234567890
stuvwxyz:;
UVWXYZ.

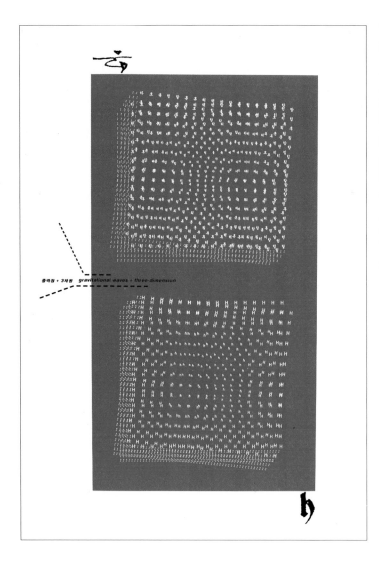

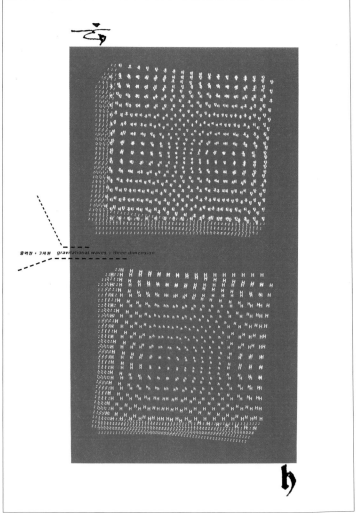

■ (PRECEDING SPREAD LEFT PAGE) **1** STUDENT: SUSANNA LEUNG COLLEGE: OTIS COLLEGE OF ART AND DESIGN DEGREE: BFA COUNTRY: USA ■ (PRECEDING SPREAD RIGHT PAGE) **2** STUDENT: DOMINIK THALE COLLEGE: BLOCHERER SCHULE DEGREE: GRAPHIC DESIGN PROFESSOR: KLAUS MÜLLER CLASS: 8TH TERM COUNTRY: GERMANY ■ (THIS PAGE) **1, 2** STUDENT: KEE-JUNG KWON COLLEGE: HONG-IK UNIVERSITY DEGREE: VISUAL COMMUNICATION PROFESSOR: SANG-SOO AHN CLASS: JUNIOR CLASS COUNTRY: KOREA

INDEX

VERZEICHNIS

INDEX

. . . .

S T U D E N T S · S T U D E N T E N · E T U D I A N T S

. . . .

COLLEGES · UNIVERSITÄTEN · UNIVERSITÉS

....

PROFESSORS · PROFESSOREN · PROFESSEURS

....

ADKINS, MARGIE TEXAS CHRISTIAN UNIVERSITY.................. 69, 155
AHN, SANG-SOO HONG-IK UNIVERSITY 214
AIKMAN, JOHN D. LINN-BENTON COMMUNITY COLLEGE 133
AKAGI, DOUG CALIFORNIA COLLEGE OF ARTS AND CRAFTS 187
AKINS, CHARLES GEORGIA STATE UNIVERSITY, ATLANTA, GA........... 157
ANDERMATT, PROFESSOR FACHHOCHSCHULE KONSTANZ, ... 138
ANDERSON, GAIL SCHOOL OF VISUAL ARTS, NEW YORK, NY 104
AUFULDISH, BOB CALIFORNIA COLLEGE OF ARTS AND CRAFTS 73
AUSTOPCHUCK, CHRIS SCHOOL OF VISUAL ARTS, NEW YORK, NY 109
AUTH, ATTILA HUNGARIAN ACADEMY OF FINE ARTS,.......... 70, 134, 184

BACICH, LEN PRATT INSTITUTE, BROOKLYN, NY 200
BAER, ROGER IOWA STATE UNIVERSITY, AMES, IA 64
BAKKOUSH, FATHI SAVANNAH COLLEGE OF ART AND DESIGN 188
BARNES, BILL O'MORE COLLEGE OF DESIGN, FRANKLIN, TN 127

BASSANI, JOHN THE SWINBURNE SCHOOL OF DESIGN 171, 185, 189
BAVIERA, PROFESSOR FACHHOCHSCHULE KONSTANZ 141
BECK, DAVID EAST TEXAS STATE UNIVERSITY, COMMERCE, TX .. 151, 161
BELIC, ZORAN MISSISSIPPI STATE UNIVERSITY 141
BERTOT, SOPHIE INSTITUT SAINT-LUC 191
BEXTE, BERND HOCHSCHULE FÜR KÜNSTE BREMEN 192
BIELENBERG, JOHN CALIFORNIA COLLEGE OF ARTS AND CRAFTS......... 135
BOSTIK, ALEX VIRGINIA COMMONWEALTH UNIVERSITY................ 128
BOSTON, ARCHIE CALIFORNIA STATE UNIVERSITY 52, 139
BRESLIN SOMMESE KRISTIN PENN STATE UNIVERSITY 20, 55, 94, 106,
.... 157, 160, 164, 173, 206, 208
BÜRK, FRITZ SCHULE FÜR GESTALTUNG BERN........................ 141

CARLSON, WAYNE THE OHIO STATE UNIVERSITY 145
CAROTHERS, MARTHA UNIVERSITY OF DELAWARE 90, 91

CALL FOR ENTRIES

STUDENT DESIGN ANNUAL 97

Entry Guidelines

By entering a Graphis competition, the sender grants permission for the attached material to be published FREE OF CHARGE in Graphis books and/or Graphis magazine published by Graphis or its licensees in print or in systems for the storage and retrieval, dissemination and reproduction of information by any means.

Eligibility

All work completed during the last academic year, including class assignments, special projects, and non-academic work.

Please send transparencies or slides of work

Preferably 2¼ x 2¼, 4x5 or 35mm. NO GLASS SLIDE MOUNTS PLEASE! Please mark the transparencies with your name and the category code that appears on the entry form. *We regret that entries cannot be returned.*

How to package your entry

Please tape (do not glue) the completed entry form (or a copy) to the back of each printed piece. For transparencies and photos just enclose the label.

Entry fees

US$ 15.00 for each single entry. US$ 35.00 for each campaign or series of three or more pieces.

A confirmation of receipt will be sent to each entrant, and all entrants will be notified shortly before the book comes off press whether or not their work has been accepted for publication. By submitting work, entrants qualify for a 25 percent discount on the purchase of the published book.

Mail entries to our New York or Zurich office:

Graphis Press, 141 Lexington Avenue, New York, NY 10016-8193
Phone: (212) 532 9387, Fax: (212) 213 3229
Graphis Press, Dufourstrasse 107, 8008 Zurich, Switzerland
Phone: (+41–1) 383 82 11, Fax: (+41–1) 383 16 43

. . . .

ENTRY DEADLINE: JUNE 1, 1996

. . . .

PLEASE TAPE (DO NOT GLUE) ON THE BACK OF EACH PRINTED ENTRY/
ENCLOSE WITH TRANSPARENCIES/SLIDES

THE ENTERED MATERIAL BELONGS TO THE FOLLOWING CATEGORY—PLEASE INDICATE THE CATEGORY IDENTIFICATION NUMBER ON LABEL AND MARK SLIDES WITH YOUR NAME

☐ 1S – ADVERTISING
☐ 2S – BOOKS
☐ 3S – BROCHURES
☐ 4S – CALENDARS/AGENDAS
☐ 5S – CALLIGRAPHY, LETTERING, TYPE
☐ 6S – COMPUTER GRAPHICS
☐ 7S – CORPORATE IDENTITY
☐ 8S – EDITORIAL/PUBLICATION DESIGN
☐ 9S – ILLUSTRATION

☐ 10S – LOGOS
☐ 11S – MULTIMEDIA
☐ 12S – MUSIC
☐ 13S – PACKAGING
☐ 14S – PRODUCT DESIGN
☐ 15S – PROMOTION
☐ 16S – SHOPPING BAGS
☐ 17S – STAMPS
☐ 18S – OTHER:_____

BRIEF INFORMATION ON ITEM:

_____

_____

STUDENT:

MAILING ADDRESS
_____

_____

TELEPHONE _____ FAX _____

COLLEGE:

ADDRESS
_____

_____

TELEPHONE _____ FAX _____

CLASS YEAR:

TERMINAL DEGREE:

PROFESSOR AND/OR CLASS (IF APPLICABLE):

_____

I HEREBY GRANT PERMISSION FOR THE ATTACHED MATERIAL TO BE PUBLISHED FREE OF CHARGE IN GRAPHIS BOOKS AND/OR GRAPHIS MAGAZINE PUBLISHED BY GRAPHIS OR ITS LICENSEES IN PRINT OR IN SYSTEMS FOR THE STORAGE AND RETRIEVAL, DISSEMINATION AND REPRODUCTION OF INFORMATION BY ANY MEANS.

SIGNATURE:

YOU MAY MAKE COPIES OF THIS ENTRY FORM.

Graphis 296

The Digital Revolution: R/GA Softimage Silicon Graphics European Mindscapes Multimedia

Graphis 295

Carson Chiat/Day Apeloig Leith Agency Legorreta Gorham

Graphis

Ishioka Fletcher Arnett ABV Achilli & Piazza CD Boxed Sets

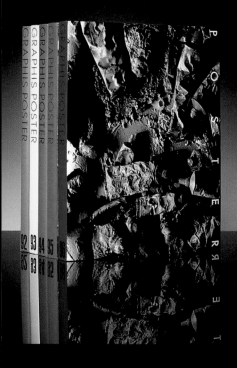

GRAPHIS POSTER
GRAPHIS POSTER
GRAPHIS POSTER
GRAPHIS POSTER
GRAPHIS POSTER

P O S T E R

92 93 94 95

The Human Condition

Photojournalism 1995

M U S I C   C D S

GRAPHIS MUSIC CDS

L O G O

GRAPHIS LOGO
GRAPHIS LOGO
GRAPHIS LOGO

1 2 3

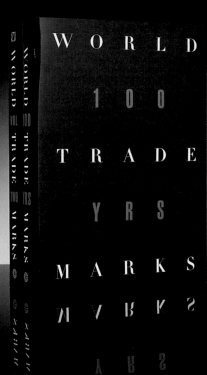

W O R L D
1 0 0
T R A D E
Y R S
M A R K S

VOL WORLD TRADE MARKS

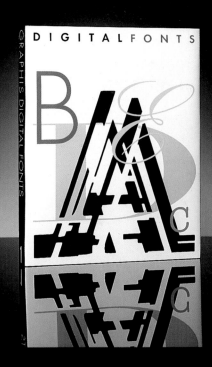

D I G I T A L F O N T S

GRAPHIS DIGITAL FONTS

B A C

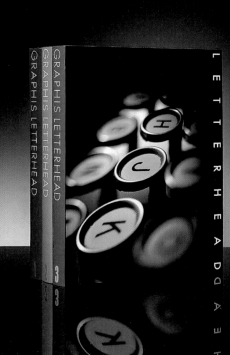

GRAPHIS LETTERHEAD
GRAPHIS LETTERHEAD
GRAPHIS LETTERHEAD

L E T T E R H E A D

3

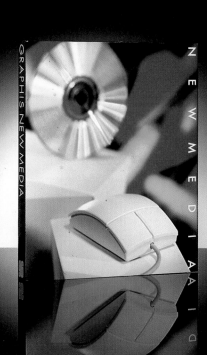

GRAPHIS NEW MEDIA

N E W   M E D I A

RICHARD SAUL WURMAN
INFORMATION
ARCHITECTS
In·for·ma·tion Ar·chi·tect [L *info-
tectus*] n. 1) the individual who
organizes the patterns inherent
in data, *making the complex
clear.* 2) a person who creates
the structure or map of information which allows others to
find their personal path to
knowledge. 3) the emerging 21st
century professional occupation
addressing the needs of the age
focused upon clarity, human understanding and the science of
the organization of information.
-In·for·ma·tion Ar·chi·tec·ture
PETER BRADFORD *EDITOR*